THE STRIP CLUB DATING SURVIVAL GUIDE

HOW TO DATE ANY EXOTIC DANCER & SURVIVE TO TELL THE TALE

BY JASON KEELER

WHEN YOU CAME IN, THE AIR WENT OUT. AND EVERY SHADOW FILLED UP WITH DOUBT.

- Jayce Everett: "Bad Things."

Copyright © 2012 by Jason Keeler

Cover & book design by Jason Keeler

Cover image of Simone DanaLustrous and Paul Ruffolo Photography

All rights reserved.

No part of this book may be reproduced in any form or by any electronic or mechanical means including information storage and retrieval systems, without permission in writing from the author. The only exception is by a reviewer, who may quote short excerpts in a review.

Jason Keeler

Printed in the United States of America

First Printing: July 2012

ISBN-13: 978-1478158233

ISBN-10: 1478158239

www.rawkmode.com

DEDICATION

This is for Seth, because nothing else matters.

And this is for Autumn, because I still remember when.

And finally, this is for you, because she's out there somewhere...

I PROMISE.

ACKNOWLEDGEMENT

*I would like to express my thanks to Simone DanaLustrous, a.k.a. Love Simone, for allowing the use of her image on the front cover, and for her insight, advice, encouragement and cruel mockery. You can sit around looking at nudie pictures of her at her totally NSFW website: **www.LoveSimone.com***

My gratitude also goes to my son's grandparents, Josh and Cheryl Taotoai, for their support during the writing process. This book never would have been written without their help, and for that I am eternally grateful.

Thanks as well to Paul Ruffolo at Paul Ruffolo Photography for being so gracious and knowing which way to point the camera; it's a rarer skill than you might think.

And special thanks to Russell Moyer Keeler, Sr. because I never really said it when I could have...I miss you Pop-Pop.

AUTHOR'S NOTE

Apparently I swear...a lot. Consider this to be your one and only warning, as well as an apology in the event any of my fucking language offends you.

Thanks for reading!

Contents

INTRODUCTION 9

ONE 28

CHAPTER 1 29
CHAPTER 2 45
CHAPTER 3 53
CHAPTER 4 65

TWO 77

CHAPTER 5 78
CHAPTER 6 86
CHAPTER 7 102
CHAPTER 8 112

THREE 118

CHAPTER 9 119
CHAPTER 10 140
CHAPTER 11 155
CHAPTER 12 170

FOUR 181

CHAPTER 13 182
CHAPTER 14 199
CHAPTER 15 206
TRUE QUOTES 218

THE STRIP CLUB DATING SURVIVAL GUIDE

HOW TO DATE ANY EXOTIC DANCER & SURVIVE TO TELL THE TALE

INTRODUCTION

I DON'T BELIEVE IT!

- Luke Skywalker: exclaiming as Yoda levitates a 15 ton X-wing fighter out of a swamp using only the power of his mind.

THAT IS WHY YOU FAIL.

- Master Yoda: explaining to Luke why he is a pussy and deserves to get his ass kicked by his own dad.

It is estimated that there are well over a quarter of a million women working in nearly 3,000 strip clubs, nude theaters, and bikini bars in the United States. That means that more than one in every thousand people, in this country, gets naked for money on a regular basis.

Nearly half of all Americans are men, and, therefore, are rather unlikely to be working as dancers in a titty bar, unless you live somewhere *unusual.* If you ignore the male population entirely, then your actual chances of encountering a woman in this country who is a stripper increase dramatically to nearly one in five hundred.

1 in 500 odds seem reasonable enough as such things tend to go, certainly a hell of a lot better than your average chance of winning the lottery. This is especially true when you stop to think that exotic dancers tend to be concentrated within

commuting distance of thousands of adult cabarets that open up for business each day all across the country.

In other words, there is a pretty significantly large population of exciting, sexually-forward, and *theoretically* single women in the business of getting naked for your entertainment concentrated in relatively predictable and fixed locations somewhere close by where you live, much to the annoyance of your wife, girlfriend or mom.

The simple fact that dancers need to be where the clubs are makes dating a stripper a straightforward matter of personal choice, taste, priorities and resourcefulness. I suspect that may seem as obvious to you as it certainly is to me, but maybe it begs the question; *why does this matter at all?*

Are exotic dancers actually the type of women that you could date? If so, would you like to? Would they want to date you? Isn't banging strippers just something that other guys say they do when they're drunk and trying to one-up each other? Does anyone actually succeed at it? Do you personally know anyone who *does?*

What value is there in learning how to approach and attract exotic dancers anyway? Aren't these girls nothing more than fantasies that exist always just beyond reach, well protected by bouncers in the club, constantly watched over by jealous boyfriends everywhere else?

Don't strippers have their own expert defenses, learned in the process of deflecting scores of horny males every night? Are strippers all hookers? Do they do porn? Will they cheat on you, or just play you for your money? Do you have to worry that your dancer girlfriend is lying to you about what she's up to every time she leaves the house?

If you can't actually have them, then what would be the point? Why even talk about it when it's not something you can have unless you're in a band or some other shit like that? Why does learning how to do it right *even matter?*

It matters because strippers are fun to hang out with in a bar, night club, your bed, her bed, someone else's bed, the back of a car, a dark alley behind the bar you were in earlier, and sometimes even in relationships, or marriage. It matters because strippers are physically fit, sexually desirable, and have flexible schedules, standards, and relationship boundaries.

It matters because strippers perform in a sexually charged, party environment, often wearing little or nothing, and seem to embrace the idea that walking around in giant platform heels with their asses hanging out somehow constitutes normal behavior. It matters because strippers shave everything, go tanning regularly, work out, and insist on sensible, work-related investments like breast enhancements.

It matters because strippers enjoy things like sex, drugs, good times, and playing dress up. It matters because strippers are skilled at entertaining, love to party, and aren't afraid to bring their girlfriends home so that you can have a new toy to play with. It matters because almost every dancer out there is, in some way or another, a lonely girl at heart.

It totally matters.

Strippers have the ability to make more money than they know what to do with, can often be found behind the wheel of cars they have no business owning, and don't mind running off to Vegas for an impromptu weekend of gambling, drinking, dancing, room service and Ecstasy fueled sex. Your stripper girlfriend will almost certainly take pleasure in helping cross out a thing or two on your *bucket list,* so long as you do her right.

The right dancer can totally captivate you, body and soul, changing how, why and what you think about almost everything. When she is pressing her body against you in the dubious privacy of some seedy strip joint VIP room, you may powerfully remember better days gone by, brighter futures and dreams long past their prime. She can drink you and your friends under the table while telling you where, and from whom, to get the best drugs.

An exotic dancer can be the principal object not only of your desire, but that of every other guy who lays eyes on her. Having a woman of this kind; this sex fantasy made tough, defensive, and unobtainable by the daily requirements of career, and lifestyle, possessing her sexually and romantically when no other man can, is the ultimate thrill in the hunt for love, sex, and partnership. The envy of your friends, as obvious as your breath on a cold winter morning, is ample reward in itself.

If that isn't enough, successfully dating just a single dancer has the effect of making you safe, approachable, and desirable to the other strippers in the club, the female staff members such as bartenders, waitresses, door and coat check girls, not to mention the attractive females at other clubs, vendors or related events.

Despite whatever vague, negative ideas that we as a society may entertain toward the idea of the adult stage performers, other females recognize the value inherent in a man that can attract and retain a woman who has a vast pool of ever changing suitors that she has rejected in his favor.

Other guys see this too, and in the end, the social significance of such a person is increased, regardless of whether we accept his girlfriend, or reject her as a whore.

As far as a stripper's physical boundaries, social mores, and behavioral modalities are concerned, the inhibitions that most women take for granted seem almost entirely, conspicuously absent. Whether by some quirk of a personal nature, a byproduct of lifestyle choices and personal style, or simply as the projection of a public persona designed to attract financial prosperity, an exotic dancer's sexuality is generally open enough that almost anything pleasurable is fair game, or close enough that it makes no practical difference.

Behaviors, requests, and the expression of fetishes in the bedroom that serve to alienate you from any other woman, or even those that can end "normal" relationships altogether are typically tolerated, if not explicitly appreciated, and encouraged.

Whether you find yourself in bed with your stripper girlfriend and her best friend at some point or not, there is always the perfect, present awareness that surprise **MÉNAGE-A-TROIS** might go down at any moment. And sometimes, it's actually just the possibility that counts, *doesn't it?*

Of course, as good as that may sound, it may be little more than an illusion, like the idea that diet Coke tastes the same as the real thing, or that the Chrysler 300 surely is every bit as enjoyable to drive as a real Bentley would be. The truth may be something a little less real than what appears on the surface, and, like the aspartame in a diet soda, leaves an aftertaste that you'll need to get used to, learn to love or to abandon altogether.

In reality, for every stripper who will never leave the house without first dressing like a supermodel, there are others who seem to possess no wardrobe beyond sweats or pajama bottoms. For each dancer who pulls up to the club in a new convertible, many more are driving cars that should not be allowed on the road in the interest of general public safety.

A dancer's permanent address is more speculative than real, residing primarily as a general idea or life expectation represented mainly by the so-called **DANCER BAGS** they haul to the club every day, and the collection of shit stuffed into the trunk of their car.

If a stripper does have a permanent place to live, it will almost always look like a bomb went off filled with dirty clothing, glitter and old food. Staples of modern life, such as primary health insurance, bank accounts, college degrees, and dads can often be things that other people have.

Many strippers are being dropped off at the club by boyfriends with whom they will spend most of the shift fighting via text message. They may be screwing the managers they work with, the bouncers that watch over them in exchange for tips or the DJs that play their music when they go on stage.

Most likely, they have a child that you haven't met yet. They use the word **FRIEND** in a way that means: *the guy I'm fucking.* They spend half their lives in the bathroom, only partially because that's usually where the **COCAINE** tends to be. Even when a dancer turns out to be legitimately single, you will, almost certainly, still get to meet their ex-boyfriend under unpleasant circumstances.

Like everyone else, strippers eventually age, become less attractive, and the demand for their company fades along with the color of their hair. Sensing that the self-centered lifestyle that defined their adulthood is rapidly drawing to a close, many dancers begin seeking validation of their youth, appeal and sexual power by sleeping with anyone and sometimes, *everyone.*

Despite all of the horrific, mind-bending torture that the average dancer is casually capable of, it may be worth remembering that the average stripper isn't some kind of soulless, shameless, immoral whore as I know it may seem, or as I may be making it sound. At least, it's *mostly* not that.

The truth is that once you've spent most of your working days trading your sexuality for rent money, jewelry from **TIFFANY** and free cell phone plans, you finally just forget how to act right, even when acting right is exactly what you've wanted all along.

You see, at some point, those old habits that once provided so much in the way of money, drugs, sex, and fun times no longer make sense anymore, because they no longer apply, and so now work against you *until the day you die.*

This might just be nature's way of keeping the scales of universal order in some kind of neat balance, proving the theory that every sin contains its own set of unique consequences, thus requires no external punishments, leaving the natural process of ecological balance and evolution provide its own.

Stripper girlfriends and all that they bring with them are pretty strong proof of that particular viewpoint on *Life, The Universe and Everything*.

It should be said, however, that these, in truth, are just the highs and the lows, the extreme consequence of an odd life, an unusual job and a social niche that places the average exotic dancer in the margin of an already dysfunctional American culture. Most of the strippers you'll actually meet are going to turn out to be relatively normal people, somewhat surprisingly.

They have families, bills, and life goals, education of some kind, hobbies, and responsibilities that are mostly taken seriously. Most of them, despite any individual challenges or personal baggage, honestly just want to live and be loved, find fulfillment, happiness, and in the end, a life worth living.

How do I know this?

I know this because strippers are what I have been doing as a lifestyle for nearly twenty years. Starting during my years serving in the Army, and continuing right up until today, I have been dating strippers and working on and off in strip clubs.

I even managed to get myself married to a stripper at one point in the course of a relationship so intense and heartfelt that *I can no longer even remember her damn name*. Take a moment and think that one over real good.

Wait a minute...actually *I do* remember her **STAGE NAME**, now that I think of it...funny, that.

Over the years, **EXOTIC DANCERS** became a staple of my dating life, and even the girls who didn't dance still tended to work in the industry as door girls, cocktail servers and bartenders. I even had a chance with a female club manager at one time, but she was so fucking hot that I didn't quite get that she was coming on to me until after I had already blown it.

After a time, however, I got sick of the bullshit and stress that often comes as a natural consequence of dating girls that are used to getting paid *every time they get naked*, and opted for a normal girl instead; the bartender working the topless joint the people who employed me had just opened up in North Hollywood.

I should mention at this point, that in my mind, *normal* in this context includes any non-stripper female who nonetheless is working at a strip club while everyone else falls into the *boring* category.

Clearly I am sick, twisted and perhaps overly concerned that my life might be deficient in **EXCITEMENT;** defined as the emotional state in which one is agitated by the immediate presence or threat of pain, suffering, distress or even death.

Still, you should know that there is a basic assumption underpinning everything I am going to say in this book; *dating girls that don't work in strip clubs is pointless because they are fucking* **DULL AS SHIT.**

Seriously now, when there are single strippers out there available to you in clubs all over the place why in the hell would you purposely pick some insipid chick who thinks that thong underwear are for sluts and *very* special occasions, and **ANAL** is something you do with your boyfriend on his birthday if he's been an exceptionally good this year?

Honestly, I'll take the crazy **MAYBE WE CAN HAVE A THREESOME TONIGHT** stripper girlfriend with all the baggage, drama and daddy issues over some lame regular girl who stuffs her fat ass into workout clothes every day even though she doesn't ever work out.

Hopefully you see where I'm coming from on this.

So, we were saying...oh, yeah I was dating a normal girl. I was with her for a few years, and things were ok. And when I say that things were ok, I mean that they were *just ok*; not only was this girl not a stripper, but she was also that odd kind of girl that works in strip clubs *and* hates strippers.

Man, what a fucking weirdo she was. But then in the last year of that relationship something else happened, something that would end up saving me from *boring*.

I met another girl.

She wasn't someone that I was dating or cheating on my girlfriend with. Perhaps saying that I had actually *met someone* might be a bit of an exaggeration since actually she was just somebody I kept running into over and over again.

I saw her working at the adult conventions, and saw her at a charity golf tournament that the southern California strip joints were putting on, and I was attending. Yes, strip clubs do put on charity events...so get over it.

One time, my *normal* girlfriend actually caught me staring at this chick, and socked me upside the head just to let me know *she meant business*. I didn't even know the name of this stupid, funny looking stripper, she was just some girl that somehow got my attention no matter how long it had been since I had seen her last.

Then one day, she and her friend came walking into the club I was managing at the time and asked to work. I remember thinking that she was the best dancer I had ever seen, and how every time she took the stage the whole club would *just stop* to watch her as she moved across the stage. Yeah, she really was that good.

And because I am completely selfish, greedy and grasping in every way, I knew I just had to have that all to myself. As I watched her from across the club, I promised myself that she would be mine...*someday.*

I remember that she wanted to go home early, and how disappointed I was that she was *one of those* skanky ass **STRIPPER-RATS** when she offered me a **PRIVATE DANCE** in the club office...*if I'd let her go.* And I remember how my disappointment abruptly faded as she started to dance for me.

If you've ever seen a girl in a white snow bunny costume and eight inch **PLATFORM STRIPPER HEELS** suddenly start *RIVER-DANCING* with enthusiasm, skill and complete commitment...well, then I suppose you can probably identify with me on this one.

If you haven't though...well, shit...seriously, you just don't know what you're missing. She even finished my "private dance" with a huge, cheesy smile and a show-stopping: "TA-DA!"

Suddenly, inexplicably...*I knew that I loved her.*

Completely disarmed; I let her leave early, swearing to myself that *some fucking how*, she would be mine.

It took a little less than six months, and required that I dump my fiancé to get there, but it was well worth it. Now, years later, our son is sitting next to me on the couch, playing *ANGRY BIRDS* on my phone as I write this.

She's off somewhere being a big-time feature entertainer and magazine model right now, and I'm writing a book. Life is kinda funny like that. My point, however, is this:

You can have the girl you want, if you want her bad enough.

At the very end of this book, I'll briefly explain something called **TDS** to you. Once you've read that and had some time to consider it, I'd suggest you come back to this dumb little story about the random girl that river danced her way into my stupid ass heart. Reread this story, and the insight you may gain about how she did it *can serve you as well.*

In addition to my own personal history dating dancers, I've spent years working at strip clubs. I've hired and fired more dancers than I can count, held their hands during breakdowns over asshole boyfriends, transitioned them from dancer to the employee and back again, written them letters of recommendation for prospective landlords and car dealers, told them to their faces that they were too fat or strung out to work, all while having innumerable heart to heart discussions with them over career, family and relationships.

I also worked for years in adult boutiques specializing in selling costumes, shoes, lingerie and accessories to strippers. I've had more girls shamelessly strip naked to try on new thong underwear, thigh high stockings and schoolgirl skirts than I ever could have thought possible back when I was a dork who couldn't get a date in high school. I have heard more ribald commentary out of the mouths of exotic dancers regarding customers, lovers and other dancers than you would possibly believe.

All the time I have spent in and around strip joints has provided me with a unique perspective on the girls that work in strip clubs, one that I am willing to share, along with all the other information that I have picked up along the way.

But how am I any different from the hundreds, perhaps even thousands of current and former strip club employees with similar experiences?

I'm still in love with the strippers.

Almost every person I ever met working in clubs eventually became jaded and bitter about his or her experiences. I would often watch in dismay as friends and co-workers quickly learned all the ways to disrespect or even hate the girls we worked with. Certainly the point of us being there in the first place were these strippers that were subject to such contempt and easy dismissal.

Maybe those people had valid reasons for the way they felt about the girls, or maybe not. I wasn't them, and it's hard to say what might be going through the minds of other assholes who aren't me. As far as I was concerned though, I had fallen in love with the girls the first time I set foot in a club, and there seemed to be no reason to change how I felt, regardless of how much **STRIPPER DRAMA**, bullshit or stupidity I ended up exposed to every day.

I think that somehow I will always be a customer at heart, always excited to see that next girl on stage, always looking forward to the fresh, new faces, and always checking my pockets to see if I have enough cash to tip or get a dance.

I presume that, if you are reading this, you are somehow, on some level, not much different, and that's alright. Loving the thrill of pursuing, dating and living with exotic dancers can be a rewarding thing, so long as you don't value life stability or your own **SELF-ESTEEM** overly much.

Strip club dating is fundamentally a **GAME** and, just like any other, it is a game with rules. If you don't know the rules, obviously you can't play. We all had to stop and read the inside of the Monopoly box the first time. Otherwise, we wouldn't have known the difference between Community Chest and Chance cards, Free Parking, and Boardwalk.

While I am certainly not claiming to be offering some definitive version of **THE STRIP CLUB RULES**, what I am giving you here might be considered a useful, abbreviated set.

My intention is not to advance some kind of step-by-step, foolproof formula for banging chicks you meet in a strip club, and surely not one that would require you to spend four hours per night, six days a week out in the field, practicing your craft. I certainly hope you didn't pick this book up thinking that's what you were getting.

What I am going to do is give you some inside information about how these clubs work, what the girls are actually like, and how you can best position yourself to maximize your enjoyment on any particular club visit, but to make yourself attractive to the girls who, as I said before, are the primary point of any strip club adventure.

THE STRIP CLUB DATING SURVIVAL GUIDE is broken up into four parts, each with a focus on one general area of information related to clubs, dancers, etiquette, money, common sense advice, strategies for success, and your own behavior.

It's set up this way specifically so that you can skip around to whatever is of most interest to you, read straight through or even return to certain parts later if you like.

In *PART ONE*, we will go on a tour of the average strip joint in America, learning a few of the basic concepts that are fundamental to the daily operation of **GENTLEMEN'S CLUBS** wherever you go.

This is a general overview that gives you a look inside the average club; just be aware that the clubs you visit in reality may be significantly different from what we talk about here depending on what type of club it is, where it is located, and what the current legal climate is like.

We'll also spend some time in that section discussing the mechanics of stripper life, where and how the money flows, and the ways that club life can impact the daily routine, worldview and expectations of an exotic dancer.

You'll have the opportunity to take a second look at life from the viewpoint of the dancer you're trying to date, perhaps finding there some insight on how to break through the typical dancer defenses and make the connection you're looking for.

In *PART TWO*, we'll take a look at some of the fundamental skills you need to have down in terms of your appearance, presentation, hygiene, social skills and common courtesy.

We will also take a moment to review some of things you just totally should not do when you're at a strip club, along with an introduction to the general rules that should govern any night out at a strip club...but which you probably *never even knew existed*.

PART THREE of the *GUIDE* will go over in some detail how to go about spending money in the club. In certain ways, nothing will be more necessary than this because every girl you'll meet is going to be in it for the money.

Knowing the correct way to handle money issues while you're at the club is the key to success when your objective is hunting the most dangerous predator species known to men:

Aurum Fossura Tripudio Meretricis.

In American English this creature is known as a *stripper*, in case you don't speak Latin. But seriously though, who *doesn't* speak Greek and Latin, am I right? I mean, what kind of society would we have if our educational system didn't teach the two languages our entire civilization was based on? That would be ridiculous...*wouldn't it?*

Why are you looking at me like that?

By the way, since we're on the subject (which we're really not, after all) why do we call it *English?* Have you ever heard *actual* English? Like...heard real English-speaking people actually speak it?

The genuine English language spoken out loud sounds like somebody from Boston caught a really nasty head cold, and now has decided to somehow rectify the situation by stuffing their mouth full of marbles while fucking a sheep. I know why and how we originally spoke English, but don't we really speak *American* now?

The one exception to this general rule about English-speaking is women from **NEW ZEALAND**. In case you're not familiar, there were these people who thought England sucked, so they went and lived in Australia, which is like Texas, but for limeys. Then some of those people were like, *"Fuck this, if I wanted to live in Texas, I'd move there,"* so they left and moved to New Zealand.

New Zealand is sort of the California of the tea and crumpet set, meaning there's gonna be a lot of hot chicks with a preference for nudity, and...oddly...crushing beer cans with their heads, although I couldn't exactly explain why. I guess in that sense it's really more specifically like Riverside (County in southern California,) only nicer.

And by *nicer*, I mean *way* nicer, and with a lot less crystal-meth and truck stops, and with a lot more towns, education, people with teeth and reasons for existing.

When these aforementioned **KIWI** girls use English it doesn't sound very much like,

"Yes, I do have a cold; why else would I have marbles in my mouth...what? Why yes, that is a sheep as a matter of fact, what of it?"

No, it doesn't sound like that at all, what it really sounds like is:

"Hey, why don't you throw me down on my surfboard and fuck me...then we'll go skiing. Wanna beer?"

Mmmmm, beer.

In *PART FOUR*, we'll discuss what happens once you've overcome those first obstacles that the woman you're pursuing will undoubtedly place in your way. As her defenses drop, the venue changes, and things start to move to another level, you'll need to learn the skills that will transform her from **SEXUAL FANTASY** into your reality. Potentially, you'll learn how to survive the experience and live to date another day.

I'm sure that almost any guy could get something of value from reading the Guide, no matter who they are, but I'm also willing to bet that if somebody already has a ton of money, looks, charisma and confidence, they likely don't need my help getting laid. I guess I should confess that *I didn't actually write this book for those guys* that already have everything.

My intention in writing this was that literally every guy, regardless of socioeconomic status, career, looks, financial worth or background can walk into any strip club, and with a little bit of work, planning and persistence can eventually walk out with a dancer on his arm.

If you have enough money, you could always just go throw that at the strippers without reading any of this, but that's not the point here at all. I want to show you how to court your **FANTASY GIRL**, work the club to your benefit, and be the guy that the girls want to go home with, all without breaking the bank, being in a rock band or resorting to *date rape drugs*.

In other words, this book is intended for use by every guy who has ever dreamed that the hot chick with the fake tits swinging around the pole could be his because she can.

She will be yours. Read on.

ONE

Knowing

CHAPTER 1

All your base are belong to us

LOOK ALIVE, MEN. I'VE GOT MY FREAK ON FOR RECON.

- George Armstrong Custer; Civil War hero, commander of the 7th Cavalry at Little Big Horn, and probable originator of the always popular, "Mustache Ride," sold, even today, for just 5 cents.

And yes, I know exactly what you're thinking; why use such an obscure quote from Custer? Well, quite simply because I'd like to emphasize the whole idea of generally knowing where the fuck you are going before you go there.

Since that's the kind of thing this whole section of the book is about actually, it seemed somewhat appropriate. Had I wanted to draw your attention to the danger inherent in underestimating your opponent, I would have probably used the other, much more famous line attributed to Custer,

"Bring the Gatling guns? What for? They're just Indians, lol!"

Of course, attempting to hook up with strippers isn't quite as much like genocidal warfare against indigenous people as you might think. Actually, it's not really like that all now that I think of it.

What? You weren't thinking that? Oh, really? Ok, well it was a dumb analogy, so shut up.

So...maybe **STRIPPER DATING** is more like a game, (does that work better for you, there Mr. Analogy Snob?) and like any game, you need to set everything up, know how all the pieces work, and learn the rules.

Maybe you sit there staring at everything that just came from inside the box as if a flash of sudden understanding will strike you from out of the clear blue sky. Then, after a few moments of feeling like a complete dumbass, you finally start looking for an instruction book or perhaps something printed on the inside of the box itself somewhere.

If you don't get the things set up properly, you can't actually play, and you can't do any of that until you've at least taken a moment to scan through the instructions. Further, figuring out how to set up the game itself gives you a vast deal more valuable insight regarding how to play, strategies for competing with the other players, and what it takes to win.

That's the most valuable thing here; that learning how this game works will provide vital information that could be the edge you'll need to outcompete the other players.

This is why the first thing we'll discuss is the setting for your game; strip clubs. They are the arena in which you will compete with other players for the ultimate prize; your own **PRIVATE DANCER** who wants to come home to you every night. The dimly lit interior of the local **CABARET** will serve as the playing field for this contest of will, cunning and stamina, thus a working knowledge of how this place works and who exactly calls it home will always be to your advantage.

You will find these places all over America; as I stated earlier, there are thousands of **LIVE ADULT ENTERTAINMENT VENUES** throughout the United States. Several hundred thousand female entertainers live within the orbit of these places.

That means that there are a *lot* of half-naked ladies are living and shaking their asses, in all likelihood, somewhere close to you.

These girls spend a considerable amount of time getting ready to go to work at the club, getting themselves to the club at the beginning of the shift, working at the club, and heading home from the club when the shift is over.

I would estimate that over half of an exotic dancer's waking hours are somehow devoted or assigned to the club in which she works, even on the days she does not physically make an appearance there.

My point is that the club your dancer works at has a tremendous impact on her life. Some of the inputs that shape the way your dancer lives her life include which goods and services are offered within the club, what kind of clientele frequent the place and the way in which the club itself categorizes and treats **ENTERTAINERS.**

The people employed at the club make decisions and take actions on a daily basis that change things for the entertainers and the rules instituted by the ownership of the club create a framework within which the daily dramas of the people who work there will play out shift after shift.

If you are planning on dating dancers then you are going to need to go find them in their natural habitat, and that's the club. Hanging out, either at coin-op Laundromats or as you cruise up and down the frozen food aisles of the grocery store is not a tactic that will work for you. If you want to succeed, you'll need to go where the girls are, and thankfully, that's going to be a strip club.

In order successfully navigate the hazardous jungle that is the inner, social structure of any given club, you will first need to get acquainted with not only the general lay of the land but the wildlife that calls this environment home.

Knowing what's up before even stepping foot in a club on your quest to meet *Ms. Right* can give you the leg up and foot in the door that will tilt the rules of the game in your favor.

First, we need to get some basic concepts regarding club life straight. The dancers, except in a very few, exceedingly rare cases, are not employees. Technically, they aren't employees of the club at all. Most strippers are a form of self-employed worker known as an **INDEPENDENT CONTRACTOR.**

This status sets dancers apart from the regular **EMPLOYEES** (managers, DJs, bouncers, bar staff, waitresses, valets, cooks, and so forth) are charged with maintaining order, overseeing the entertainment, providing customer service, handling food and beverage sales and so on.

Despite this putative **SELF-EMPLOYED** status, however, the dancers are constantly directed and supervised by club employees, typically the management staff who are acting as agents of the proprietor, partnership or corporation that owns the joint.

As a **CUSTOMER,** working game on the dancers, it can be tremendously helpful to understand the limitations and constraints under which the club, employees and dancers are operating. Oftentimes the set of local laws that govern the club you hang out at are Byzantine in the extreme.

At best, these regulations are intended to keep any unlawful monkey business from happening and, at worst, intended to make it impossible to operate a profitable adult business at all.

While the operation of most adult businesses is protected under both the U.S. and various state constitutions, there is no law anywhere that says that the authorities need allow conditions to exist that might ensure that those same businesses can become, *or remain*, profitable.

This means that an unending series of hurdles that a strip club needs to surmount on an ongoing basis in order to remain in operation. The part here that you need to get is that all this legal bullshit tends to translate downwards to set a policies and processes governing behaviors inside the club that must be respected.

So, despite the fact that the entertainer that you have a crush on is not an employee, and is technically her own boss, *she still has to do what she is told* by club staff and management, as well as keep her conduct within the boundaries of club protocol, etiquette and best practices, none of which she has any control over.

This all sort of brings us, in a roundabout way, to the topic of you getting laid actually *at or inside* a strip club, something that is just about as likely as getting hit by lightning or winning the lottery. That is to say that it *can happen*, and it certainly *does happen*, but I wouldn't go holding my breath waiting for it.

The aforementioned adult business regulations and all the structure that is created within adult clubs to police things make something like this a fairly rare occurrence. This is almost rare enough to say that it never happens but of course I think we are all adult enough here to recognize "never" is a pretty powerful word when the context is naked girls, horny men, liquor, loud music and a dark, intimate location. Still, I wouldn't bother counting on it, even if you are filthy rich and willing to spend money as if it's going out of style.

It's not just Johnny Law standing in the way of you scoring some pussy at the club either. Fact is these girls aren't hookers. Yeah, maybe they don't mind using their **SEXUAL NATURE** and their bodies to their own advantage when the issue is economic gain but that doesn't mean they're a bunch of ratty street walkers.

Mostly, these are normal women we're talking about. They want sex with men that they are genuinely attracted to and with whom they feel safe, secure and comfortable. Just because you toss a couple of twenties their way and grab your crotch suggestively don't go expecting them to get all wet and willing. They may pretend that a guy acting like some pubescent cave man is what gets them hot, but that's just because it's their job *to make you think that*. Don't fool yourself on this point or you will go making a fool out of yourself.

SOLICITING SEX from the entertainers in a strip club is a sure fire method to get shunned by everyone there, if not asked or even forced to leave altogether. Asking dancers to meet you off premise, at a motel or your apartment is not getting you anywhere either. Neither should you waste time asking the girls if they do **PRIVATE PARTIES** or any of that other crap; they hear that kind of thing all the time and they'll see you for what you are; your rotted soul and withered, black excuse for a heart will give you away as the motherfucker that you truly are. Just realize that until you succeed in pulling the girl from the club altogether, you aren't getting to screw her.

Plus, your goal here is not to fuck dancers just to do it, although that will certainly come in time. Your goal here is presumably to form actual, ongoing relationships with one or more of them and, somehow, survive the experience. The kind of dancer that would go off premise with you for money is obviously not the kind of girl you should look for. Save yourself some time and trouble on this one and just assume, whether it is true or not, that the answer is always *no*.

Some of the basic preliminaries are now out of the way, let's meet people and players that have such an effect on the dancer you are pursuing, or planning to. The following people comprise the basic cast and crew of any strip club:

Owner

Manager

VIP Host

Bouncer

Bar Staff

House Mom

House Dancer

Feature Entertainer

There may be other players depending on what kind of club you frequent and where it is located such as valets, door girls, coat check girls, cooks and restroom attendants. For our purposes, however, these people will have far less impact on the girl you are seeking, therefore, I will simply categorize them collectively as **SUPPORT STAFF** and deal with them separately. And when I say, *deal with them separately*, I mean *ignore them entirely*. Just know that these people exist in many club environments and that you should handle them politely, with respect and **REMEMBER TO TIP**, when appropriate.

OWNERS

There are quite a few strip clubs out there that might be what you call a **MOM AND POP** operation. That is to say that they are owned and operated by a single person, usually a man, a married couple or perhaps a small, limited partnership.

In some cases, the individual club is part of a small or regional chain operation, and there will be a district or regional manager taking the place of the owner who is running things from out of the area. In a few instances, the club will be part of a national chain, and this can create all sorts of odd ownership arrangements.

Some are partnership driven; some are licensing arrangements, and others are publicly traded on the stock market. In a club of this kind, there is no clearly defined individual owner as such, but there are quite a few people in charge with **VIP STATUS** and a certain amount of personal juice.

MANAGERS

You are unlikely to interact directly with any people representing ownership on a regular, ongoing basis unless they are the mom-and-pop type club. In this case, the actual owner is often on premise operating the business, and you may get to know them for whether you want to or not.

In most cases, however, you will be dealing with ownership via their paid agents: the club General Manager and his or her assistant managers usually referred to as shift managers.

The **GENERAL MANAGER (GM)** acts as the primary representative of the owner and is the central authority in the day-to-day operations of the club. They can often be found inhabiting the day shifts at the club since this is what the rest of the world considers normal business hours.

They are charged with all of the administrative tasks of the club such as labor scheduling, payroll, dealing with vendors, hiring/firing of staff, communicating with the ownership of the club, supervising the other managers, and directly managing the shifts that they are working on.

The **SHIFT MANAGERS** (there are usually at least two of these) are technically subordinate to the GM and cover the night and weekend shifts. While they may have some additional club-level responsibilities, the primary role of the shift manager is direct supervision of the shifts he or she is assigned to.

They tend to handle most of the meaningful entertainer interactions, and are often responsible for scheduling the majority of the dancer shift appearances.

Unless the club is set up in such a way as to require the GM to work or be present during prime night shifts, this territory will be the domain of the most successful and typically senior Shift Manager.

This manager will be in direct control of the shifts with the most paid staff assigned, the greatest number of entertainers in attendance and the busiest customer traffic. It will usually also be these shift periods that are home to noteworthy events, contests or discount sales.

So, while the GM is the titular head of the club management structure, the night managers are actually in control of most of the employees, dancers, customers and promotions. This creates all sorts of tension within the management structure, and there may be some kind of factional infighting going on within the club social circles.

Some club organizations recognize the issue and attempt to compensate for it, and some don't. Either way, you should be aware that this kind of thing can exist at the club you go to, and you should take no part in it.

Strip clubs tend to incubate all sorts of dramatic behavior that you probably haven't seen since you left high school. Juvenile, petty and hurtful things can happen in a heartbeat. Staying out of it is to your benefit.

Remember that your purpose here is not to get caught up into some type of real life soap opera but to have a terrific time while meeting girls. Getting involved in gossip, taking sides, conspiring, and backstabbing all work at cross purposes to your own goals. Stay out of it, stay clean and keep your eyes on the prize: the hot ass chick in the flimsy lingerie.

If you are interacting with the GM of the club, act like it. He or she is the person who has been placed in charge of the club by its owner, and should be accorded a level of respect commensurate with that position. On the other hand, if you are talking to the manager who controls most of what actually goes on in the club by virtue of working the prime shifts, feel free to treat them according to what they are: the management employee entrusted with handling the strongest money-making time slots.

These people are necessary to the optimum operation of the club, and you should be on excellent terms with all of them, as well as anyone else involved in a management function. It honestly should not matter to you what these people think of each other, or if they are engaged in some kind of pointless internal power struggle.

Just treat them all with respect, smile when you see them, shake hands firmly, and always look them in the eyes. Always treat people you meet in the club just as you would like to be treated yourself and you'll be Ok.

VIP HOST

While there will always be an owner, a GM, and one or more Shift Managers, the club you go to may or may not have what is usually referred to as a **VIP HOST.** This person is often an hourly or salaried employee but can just as easily be working on commission or even be acting as an independent contractor.

The purpose of the VIP Host is to ensure a steady flow of high-value customers to the club and, at the other end, to make sure that those customers are receiving the best possible treatment, the most preferential seating, the best girls and a steady flow of overpriced bottle service, cigars, food or whatever else.

VIP hosts may act in the role of party planner, handle custom preparation of prime seating, schedule entertainers to ensure the highest level of VIP guest satisfaction, deliver flowers or gifts, run certain types of errands or act as matchmaker not only between guests and the entertainers, but as a networking conduit between the best customers.

While the VIP Host is a terrific person to know, you should remember that most of what they do comes with a price whether it's for the sale of a high-priced service or item, or a straight tip for services rendered.

BOUNCERS

The next three people to know about are the floater, the floor man and the door man. These positions are generally functions of the on-staff security as opposed to being specific job descriptions.

The **FLOATER** is the bouncer working the private dance area, watching out for the girls, making sure you pay for your dances and arbitrating any disputes that come up. This is the guy that you will tip to look the other way if you have an especially friendly dancer sitting in your lap during a private dance.

The **FLOOR MAN** is the bouncer that is walking the main showroom floor and patrolling the open areas of the club. In most clubs, there will be more than one person doing this job.

The role of the floor man is to watch out for problems in the main public areas of the club and stop them before getting out of hand. If you ever see someone being removed from a strip club, it is most likely the floor men who are taking out the trash.

Conversely, this is the person to go to if some kind of issue arises within the club and you require assistance. Whether it is some drunken asshole starting a problem, or just that you seem to have misplaced your cell phone, wedding ring, or wallet, it will usually be the Floor Man that will be there to sort it out.

The **DOORMAN** is just what he sounds like, the guy who watches the door. This tends to be the bouncer on the low end of the totem pole, perhaps because he is new and inexperienced or because the other security staff members have trust issues with him. This guy also tends to get the short end when the tips are shared out at the end of the shift, so dropping a couple of bucks on him when you arrive at the club will make him a fast friend. Doesn't have to be much, it's the consideration that counts here.

BAR STAFF

There will always be people operating some sort of bar arrangement, even if it is the kind of club that can't serve alcohol (usually fully nude clubs.) In that case, there may be a single person acting as a **BARTENDER/WAITRESS** serving you dramatically marked up juice, soda and energy drinks.

Other places will be offering a full bar with all the amenities and plenty of bartenders, cocktail servers, and bar backs to make sure that you are never sitting there with an empty glass.

In any case, there will always be staff members assigned to take care of refreshments and provide service at your table or booth. These people will almost always have considerable information on the dancers that work the club so you will need to stay on favorable terms with them.

This can often be a pleasant task since the bar staff is usually composed of attractive women in their own right. Information flows two ways as well, so if you act like an ass with the bar staff they are almost sure to tell the dancers. You should always remain on your best behavior since there undoubtedly is no need to make your life any harder than it.

Another thing you should probably know about the bar staff, **BARTENDERS** in particular. Just like the entertainers, the bar and wait staff are usually hot females who are making a respectable living off their looks. Also like the dancers, the bar and wait staff cultivate customers who they are prone to become territorial over.

This can even lead to competition between the staff and the entertainers prized **MONEY CUSTOMERS**. You may find dancers and bartenders taking turns gossiping with you about each other, making accusations, and generally trying to turn you against their rivals.

Once again, you must not allow yourself to be drawn into these soap opera games and intrigues. I can't tell you how many customers get pulled into these things thinking that they have some inside information and walking around all flattered and "in the know." They don't know shit, trust me. Stay out of this kind of thing, always.

Let them fight over you and anyone else that they want but don't allow it to have any significant impact your behavior. Stay friendly with the bar staff, be courteous, tip and focus on the dancers that are unquestionably the point of you being in the club in the first place.

You may just find that if you simply treat the staff appropriately you will be treated better in return. With all the guys sniffing around the bar staff trying to get laid, just acting "normal" can tend to make you more appealing.

HOUSE MOM

Another person that may or may not be present depending on the club you are at is the **HOUSE MOM**. Sometimes there are more than one of these, and they are occasionally male (referred to as a "Houseparent.")

The purpose of the House Mom is to handle issues in the entertainer dressing area. She keeps people from stealing, prevents fights, acts as the representative of management in the dressing room and sells odds and ends (Band-Aids, tampons, nail polish, Tylenol) to the entertainers.

The House Mom also has a role to play in the way the dancers look as they enter and leave the dressing area.

Dancers usually need to pass by the House Mom who will check their nails, hair and costume to ensure that they meet the appearance standards that the club requires when appearing before the customers. Some House Moms also make a reasonable living selling dancer clothes and shoes to the girls.

Since the House Mom hears almost everything that goes on in the dressing room, they are privy to a lot of "girl talk." They will know about any customers of note, and have a clear line on who to talk to and who to ignore. You may or may not ever get the chance to interact with the House Mom under normal circumstances, but it pays to remember that she is somewhere in the back of the club both hearing *and* telling all.

That's just about everyone you'll find in the average strip joint except for the dancers themselves, and they get their own chapter, next.

CHAPTER 2

Girls, girls, girls

DON'T LAUGH; YOUR DAUGHTER MIGHT BE WORKING HERE.

- Sign posted outside a strip club in South Dakota.

This brings us to the entertainers. The exotic dancers you will find in gentlemen's clubs come in two basic forms, House Dancers and Feature Entertainers. House dancers are the workaday, 9-5 girls.

They normally live somewhere nearby the club; are well known to the staff, other entertainers and the customers. They have regulars that they depend on seeing as often as possible, and consider this club to be their home base.

HOUSE DANCERS

A **HOUSE DANCER** is paying "hard" fees to the club for the right to work there (a subject I will cover in detail in another section.) Additionally, they are paying "soft" fees in the form of regular tip percentages to the in-house staff. These dancers are usually obligated to somewhat theoretical performance schedules dictating what shifts they will work at the club.

They appear on stage at regular intervals during the shift as required by management and under the supervision of the club DJ.

FEATURE ENTERTAINERS

Headline dancers brought in by the club for specific events are known as **FEATURE ENTERTAINERS.** They are contracted through adult talent agencies like the Continental Agency, the Lee Network, A-List Features, and Pure Talent Agency, amongst others. The purpose of a feature entertainer's show is usually to drive business during down times, pull customers from the competition on one of their high traffic days or act as the centerpiece of some kind of event like a grand opening, anniversary or holiday party.

Generally, features fall into one of four categories:

Porn Stars

Show Girls

Freak Shows

Celebrities

PORN STARS

The most common form of feature act these days are Porn Stars. While some of these girls possess true name recognition and a built in draw, the fact that they are in porn does not actually mean that they can pack the house.

In fact, the absolute glut of starlets out there and the production values inherent in today's **GONZO** porn industry tends to insure that quite a few of the girls working the feature circuit as porn stars are mostly unknown.

Worse still, most porn starlet features apparently couldn't dance worth a shit if their lives depended on it, seemingly lack any ability or desire to put on a decent show or even bother to stay sober during their appearance.

That leaves you, the customer, paying heavily inflated prices at the door and bar to see some girl you've never heard of roll around on stage like a clumsy wreck in a cheap, one-size-fits-all costume that was clearly purchased online.

At one time in the club industry, feature entertainers had played a vital role, bringing new costumes, dance routines, games and a level of excitement that would be hard to maintain with just the on-hand, in-house dancers. They also provided a central focus for marketing and promotions in the club, essentially giving the club a new story to tell its customers with each new feature event. As a bonus, a skilled feature dancer often had the ability to inspire the resident house girls to up their game in terms of appearance, costumes and stage performances.

The current domination of low-grade porn star features has made an end to all that, however. The lack of reliability, poor show date performances, unrealistically high appearance fees and low customer turnout associated with porn stars has nearly killed the entire feature segment of the adult club industry.

Club owners and managers all over the country have practically opted out of the feature game, tired of all the hassle, expense and low returns, almost exclusively due to the primacy of the porn star feature.

SHOWGIRLS

Showgirls, on the other hand, are dancers who normally have spent some considerable time dancing in clubs as house girls and have little or no experience in the porn industry. These are typically strippers who want to make a career out of exotic dancing but know that their productive time in clubs is somewhat limited. For them, featuring is like career progression, offering financial rewards and recognition not available to girls that never leave the club environment.

SHOWGIRL features tend to emphasize elaborate costumes, onstage props, some degree of dance choreography (and expertise to back it up) special effects, unique skills and customer interaction games.

Most of them spend considerable time working the **CONTEST CIRCUIT**, using their victories as a means for establishing *marketable credits* that will make them attractive hires for club owners.

FREAK SHOWS

Freak Shows commonly involve midgets, but there are also "fat lady" freak shows, as well as girls with freakishly large breasts and shows featuring twin sisters. There are a few performers out there that do a sort of onstage **DOMINATRIX** gig, and I suppose those would count as freak shows too.

Despite what you might think, or perhaps *confirming* your worst fears, **FREAK SHOWS** tend to be the most popular kind of feature event booked these days.

I personally oversaw several of them and even put together a "fat lady versus midget" event at one point. It was wildly successful to nobody's immense surprise.

CELEBRITIES

Finally, there is the newest feature category, the **CELEBRITY** feature. These "features" sometimes will perform as do the other feature types, but many of them take the form of an on-site appearance rather than an actual performance.

Examples of Celebrity features would include somebody who gained fame from reality television, were the less-famous partner in somebodies leaked sex tape or became known as the mistress that broke up some famous guy's marriage.

In short, so-called Celebrity features are generally obnoxious bores with an astonishing short shelf life and little to no actual draw in a gentleman's club.

I'm not exactly clear on who originally thought this semi-celebrity snake oil was such a brilliant idea, but I have yet to see one of these events work to the benefit of the club and its customers.

The Internet is already full of enough pictures of self-centered drunk girls striking "duck face" poses without you driving down to a strip joint to meet them in person. Avoid these feature events if the club you frequent is foolish enough to pay for them.

STAR FUCKING

The amount of time that you might be in contact with any particular feature dancer is so limited that your opportunity for any meaningful interactions is severely limited. Even if you could quickly hook it up with a porn starlet why would you want to? Are you planning to date her?

Before sticking a toe in those waters, I would simply draw your attention to the fact that *she has sex with other men in public for money*. Maybe you're into that, but for most guys, I think the stress of such a relationship would be too much to bear.

The show girls seem like a better group, many of them are intelligent and hard-working and, despite the fact of what they do for a living, they aren't cheap whores. For the most part, they are actually just *souped-up* versions of the girls you are already chasing in the club, so what's the problem?

Well, most of them have moved on from the night-to-night, hand to mouth existence of the strip club and are now moms, wives, committed girlfriends or fiancés. They are seeking stability, advancement and career success. Hooking up with some customer they encounter during the course of a three or four day feature assignment seems counterproductive to their life goals just to put it mildly.

Could there be any "heart of gold" porn starlets just looking to meet the right guy (namely you) and leave it all behind them for a new life of monogamous bliss? Sure there are. Are there also show girls whose selfish nature and limited sense of commitment drive them to hit it with anyone possessing a heartbeat and a penis after a couple of glasses of cheap chardonnay? Yes, of course there are. I wouldn't go betting the farm on you meeting one of them and being *the guy* though.

What about the freak shows? Well, that all depends on you doesn't it? Do you like midgets and tremendously fat girls? Oddly, most of the "freak" features tend to be married and bring their husbands along to the show in the role of **HANDLER/PROTECTOR.**

I suppose it takes all kinds to make the world go round. I would suggest to you that if that if people with unusual physical characteristics, like being a dwarf, are your thing, there are probably better, saner places to meet them than a strip joint. Plus, midgets drink a lot. I mean a lot. Like more than you can imagine. Things can get ugly quick when you are dealing with a **DRUNKEN MIDGET IN A THONG.**

That just leaves the "Celebrity" feature. At least here you often have a point of reference. All you have to do is go back and watch reruns of the inane reality show that she was on at one point in her life and see if the person you see there is truly someone you'd like to have a truly rewarding and intimate relationship with.

Can you imagine, having to hold her hair out of the way while she vomits up tequila for the third time in the past twenty-four hours, facing off with her ex-boyfriend in the parking lot of a bar or picking her up from jail again?

Think all that over carefully before deciding whether or not it would be worthwhile to get involved. Then, regardless of whatever it was you decided there, stay far, far away and let them be some other moron's problem.

The bottom line here is that you should not categorize Feature Entertainers as being people you are seeking relationships with. There are just too many factors working against you for it to be worth the time.

The only real exception I will make to this is in the event that you are dating a stripper who is staying in the business, and at some point decides to move into Showgirl featuring.

This brings us to the House Dancers who are the real meat-and-potatoes of any strip joint. These are the girls that you will see any time you go into the club.

They are the girls you are most likely to have the opportunity to form relationships with since they will be the dancers most available and accessible to you on an ongoing basis. We'll take a closer look at house dancers in the next chapter.

CHAPTER 3

If it doesn't make dollars, it doesn't make sense

STRIPPERS ARE PEOPLE, TOO. NAKED PEOPLE, WHO MAY BE WILLING TO PLEASURE YOU FOR A PRICE YOU NEGOTIATE LATER, BEHIND A CURTAIN IN THE VIP ROOM.

- Alexander Hamilton: Founding Father, Secretary of the Treasury in Washington's Cabinet; died after a duel with a political rival upon whom he had talked mad shit during the 1800 elections; thus proving that our nation was built by some badass motherfuckers.

As I have said previously, house dancers are where the rubber meets the road in strip clubs. They are what you are thinking of when the word stripper comes to mind. These are the girls that I assume you are trying to date if you are reading this, so they are the ones you should come to know best.

House dancers come in just about as many shapes and sizes as you can imagine. I have seen the most startlingly beautiful women grace the stages of various **GENTLEMEN'S CLUBS**, only to be then followed in quick succession by women who have no business leaving their house, let alone getting naked in public.

The temperament of the average club entertainer runs the full gamut as well, from aggressive, **BIPOLAR** nightmares to meek, trusting damsels in distress. Trying to outline who or what defines a stripper is nearly *impossible*.

Instead, let me give you the rundown on how things work in the club for dancers, and perhaps then you'll begin to see how they might then translate that reality into the way they are dealing with you.

RENT

As we have discussed, strippers are rarely club employees. They are almost always something known as an independent contractor. What this means is that the entertainers essentially work for themselves, theoretically *renting space* from the club.

For the purposes of some masturbatory abstraction of theoretical economics, there is a presumption that strippers have a unique service to offer (their dance performances), but they need some kind of facility in which to market and sell their service.

Strip clubs assume all of the cost and risk involved with permitting, legal compliance, advertising, security, insurance, marketing and promotions, labor costs, facility maintenance, management overheads, utilities and consumables like alcohol and food.

All of this costs considerable sums over time, which are covered with door charges on the customers, ATM fees, sales of food and drink, merchandise sales, special fees on dances and an elaborate structure of rents, percentages and charges levied against the entertainers that wish to use the club.

The fees and financial obligations owed by a dancer to the club she works in are often collectively referred to as **TAXES**. In other words, the amount of money she earns is a gross, just like for normal wage earners like you and me, her real income is the net amount she makes it home with after paying everything and everyone out at shift end.

This does not even take into account *real taxes* that she owes to the federal and state tax collectors, amounts that will largely remain unpaid.

I want to note here that how this all works varies tremendously from club to club. Some clubs will charge more or less, pay the dancers or simply charge them nothing. There may be significant variety in how this kind of thing is handled, but again, this should represent the average situation.

RENT: STAGE FEES

That said, strippers usually get taxed in four different categories; stage fees, often referred to as rent, fees on dances, tip-outs, and tips for service. Stage fees are charged to the entertainers for the right to use the club, its infrastructure and staff. This can either be a flat fee or something keyed to how desirable the shift is.

An example of this would be a club that charges a dancer $20 if they arrive for work anytime between when the club opens and 8PM, $40 if they arrive between 8PM and 10PM or $60 for the right to show up after ten.

Clubs tend to charge an escalating fee like this because it encourages girls to show up on the slow times, like the day shifts. They can gradually increase the fees as it gets later because the club knows that dancers will be showing up to work the busy nights no matter how much they are being charged.

Stage fees may be as low as $10 or $20, but in prime markets, such as the clubs in Las Vegas, a $70–$100 fee might be considered a bargain.

Some clubs will require the entertainers to pay up front before ever being allowed access to the main showroom and the customers there, while other clubs collect the fee at the end of the dancer's shift.

RENT: DANCE FEES

Some clubs will also be charging dance fees against the stripper's take on the action that happens in the club's various dance areas. In some cases, this will be a flat fee, other times it may be a percentage of the total earned.

As I have already noted, this may not be common practice in every club, but it is common enough to mention here. This portion of the fee structure can end up amounting to quite a bit of money depending on how the club handles it.

For example, if a club is charging a $50 stage fee and a 20% Dance Fee, and an entertainer racks up 25 dances at $20 a pop for a total of $500, then her payout to the club at the end of the shift would be $150:

$50 stage fee + $100 dance fee [$500 x .20 = $100] = $150

This leaves the dancer with $350 take home out of what she earned during the shift. While this does not take into account any tips or money she made dancing on stage, $150 is still a considerable chunk to lose before you even walk out the door. And we haven't even accounted for tip outs yet, another thing that tends to bleed the dancers half to death on the way home.

TIPS

Of course, dancers have to tip all the time. Tips come in two basic forms: tip outs and **TIPS FOR SERVICE**. The latter of the two is just what it sounds like, tipping for services that occur during the shift.

 An example of this would be someone on staff getting tipped out by a dancer for putting them on to a paying customer, helping settle a money dispute in the dancer's favor, the bar staff or VIP Host giving extra attention to an entertainer's best customer or the manager spending an hour searching for, and recovering, a lost purse or cell phone.

While tips for service are just considered proper etiquette and good karma, **TIP OUTS** are an unofficial requirement. Most of the time, clubs have some kind of semi-official tip out threshold, somewhere in the 15–20% range. This is how it works: at the end of shift, a dancer owes the DJ a minimum tip equal to 10% or greater of the total amount of money earned before the club takes a cut.

TIPS: THE DJ

Earlier I gave an example of a girl who made $500 in dances, remember? Let us just imagine that she also made about $100 in tips while dancing on stage, so she has a total of

$600 in income. She owes her DJ an absolute minimum of $60 [10% of $600] which, if that is what she hands him at the end of the night, will cause her to be viewed as a cheap bitch and liable to receive absolute minimal service from that DJ on the next shift that they work together. He'll tell everyone working that night what a cheap bitch she is, and most likely attempt to get the manager to do something about it next time she comes in.

TIPS: THE BOUNCERS

In addition to the tip out to the DJ, the entertainers are also expected to hit the bouncers with a 5–10% tip that will normally be shared equally among them. So again referring to our example dancer with $600, the security tip would be $30–$60 depending on the expectations at the club. That amount will be shared out between all the bouncers as I said, meaning that if there are six bouncers splitting $60, then the most anyone can expect to get is $10.

Of course, if you have twenty or thirty girls handing you $10 every night as they walk out to the parking lot these amounts can add up quickly to a new car or a down payment on a house. Failing properly to tip the security guys can not only result in shitty treatment (see *DJ, above*) but may also result in an entertainer not getting backed up at a critical moment during some future shift.

TIPS: THE MANAGER

Although it almost never falls within any kind of official tip out policy, in many clubs the strippers are expected to tip out to the management along with everyone else. Some clubs explicitly prohibit tips to managers from dancers since this *might compromise* management integrity (seriously) instead choosing to force employees to share a portion of the tips they get from the entertainers with their shift manager.

It probably goes without saying that this is at least unethical if not strictly illegal. The staff can ensure that the manager will always take their side in a dispute over tips if they share with him, or at least that's the general idea. Regardless of how it all goes down though, this is just a shrewd trick that club owners use to get around having to pay managers properly.

So let's put this all together using the hypothetical stripper who just pulled that $500 worth of dance money and $100 on stage. She is going to pay out $120 in tips, half to the DJ and the other half to the bouncers, leaving $480.

We already set the stage fee at $50, and the dance fee at 20%, for a total of $150 in club fees, which leaves our girl with $330. Let's say that she is accustomed to tipping her manager 5% (in this case $30), so she has $300 *after taxes*.

While I am by no means trying to suggest that making $300 for a work day lasting anywhere from 4-8 hours is bad money, you should try to remember what an exotic dancer is doing for that money. Getting naked for strangers, feigning sexual interest in people that she at best couldn't care less about, being in intimate physical contact with often unattractive customers with foul breath or body odor, being groped, intimidated, sexually assaulted, and bored to death by idiot drunks are all par for the course on any given day.

Of course, we should all recognize that this is the life that these girls choose, and they are getting compensated for it, often quite well. That, however, doesn't actually make it any easier. If you have some idea that the dancers are living out a cushy, fantasy existence filled with sex, excitement and practically free money, you couldn't be farther from the truth. Again, this is their choice, not something being forced on them, but it pays to remember that *this shit isn't easy* for anyone.

WORKING GIRLS, PART ONE

When dancers arrive for their shift they are normally required to check-in with the manager on duty, letting him or her know that the performer is on premise. In some clubs, this is the point at which the stage fee is paid. Afterward, the entertainer will spend some time getting prepared for her shift in the club dressing room.

Depending on the entertainer and what her day looked like prior to arriving, this period may last anywhere from just a few minutes to several hours. Most girls seem to take 45 minutes to an hour to go from walking into the club wearing sweats and a t-shirt to heading onto the showroom floor in a bikini and platform heels.

Once girls are on the floor, they are usually expected to check-in with the DJ, although how this is handled will vary markedly from club to club. Some places have an automated system that notifies the DJ once the dancer has checked in, but in most places, you wouldn't know a girl has arrived until she walks up to the sound booth and announces herself.

TWO MINUTES, THIRTY SECONDS

While we're sort of touching on the subject of DJs and all that, I'd like to make mention here of the idea of song length, and what it means to you as a guy enjoying himself in a strip club. While you may not realize it, hearing a full length song in a strip club is pretty damn rare. Most clubs aim for a **STANDARD SONG LENGTH OF TWO MINUTES, THIRTY SECONDS.**

This is intended to ensure that things sort of move along nicely, because, believe it or not, it can get downright boring if the same girl is on stage too long. Also, and in some ways more importantly, this is designed to keep the length of songs in the dance area as standard as possible.

Knowing this little fact can also be helpful to you as a customer in the event you do something stupid, like trying to dispute how much you owe for the dances you just got in the VIP. When you are dealing with the bouncer and attempting to explain to him that it was only three songs and not the four that the dancer is claiming, I want you to remember that *he knows* how many you owe.

Why? Because five minutes equals two dances, ten minutes are equal to four dances, and an hour is twenty-four dances. *He's not guessing how many you did, you are.* So stop looking like a chump, pay the lovely lady, and make your exit gracefully. Tomorrow you can call your mom and borrow money for rent. You'll live.

WORKING GIRLS, PART TWO

Once the entertainers have checked in with the DJ they are generally free to do as they like so long as they aren't breaking any laws or violating club rules and they remain responsive when the DJ calls them to the stage. This is the point when a dancer will first begin to approach customers, get her first set on stage over with and, if the joint serves alcohol, probably hit up the bar for a shot just to get things going.

This first appearance on the main showroom floor is usually a dicey point for any girl's psyche and has the potential to sort of set the tone for the rest of the shift. Most of the entertainers will be undergoing some kind of anxiety at this point, and experience what is known as, **APPROACH AVOIDANCE**. That works like this:

A dancer is standing alone out in the open in a heavily air-conditioned room, inundated with the babble of indistinct conversations of customers and dancers, the blaring of the sound system, the flashing stage lighting, and the clear awareness that she is practically naked. As she makes her way onto the floor, people will pause what they are doing to turn and stare at her, even if only for a moment.

They will look her over, openly judge her with their eyes, and turn back to their friends to critique her physical features and level of attractiveness. The dancer will often overhear nearby customer conversations featuring loud, specific commentary regarding her suitability as a sexual partner, *or lack thereof*.

BAD DREAMS

Remember those dreams you used to have as a kid when you would show up late to class on the day of the final math test only to discover that you had forgotten to get dressed and were standing in front of your teacher and classmates totally in the buff? As if this dream doesn't suck enough already, the other students would usually be making fun of you as you stood there, powerless to run away or cover yourself. Then, *because fate is fucking cruel*, you would wake up to your beeping alarm only to realize you had to get up for school because you did, in fact, have a significant math test that day.

Regardless of whether you ever had that specific dream or not (*quit lying, everybody had that fucking dream*), you almost certainly suffered through something similar enough that you can identify with it. Recall the feelings this dream could create in you; **FEAR, SELF-LOATHING, HELPLESSNESS, PANIC, GENERALIZED ANXIETY.** Imagine having to live through that dream in a waking state, otherwise known as *real life*, every time you went to work.

Think about that for a moment. Imagine that every day, when you get up and go to work, you would have to stand in front of the class naked while people say things out loud about you that they would never, ever say in any other situation at all.

This somewhat approximates what a stripper goes through every time she walks out into the showroom at the start of her shift. It can be psychologically destructive and frankly terrifying, and it happens *every single time* she shows up to work.

Once the girl is out on the floor she now has to approach customers. Remember that dancers are essentially **SALES PEOPLE**, and if they don't talk to anyone there is *no way* for them to make money. As I've just explained though, a dancer

63

just hitting the floor is rarely in any position to go hit up some stranger with any sense of true **PERSONAL POWER.**

Thus, strippers will often sort of mill about for a bit in an attempt to avoid directly confronting the customers until their comfort level rises high enough to overcome their anxiety driven paralysis. This is the *approach avoidance* that I mentioned earlier.

In the next section we will discuss how a dancer's psychological distress and coping mechanisms like *approach avoidance* present you with an opportunity to be more than just some dumbass customer waving dollar bills around.

CHAPTER 4

Crazy bitch

WHEN THE WORLD SLIPS YOU A JEFFREY, STROKE THE FURRY WALL.

- Abraham Maslow, American professor of Psychology once labeled mentally unstable during a childhood psychological evaluation, considered to be the founder Humanistic Psychology and first described the concept of The Hierarchy of Needs. Really knew how to say, "Go fuck yourself" creatively.

It doesn't matter who you are, where you come from or where you are going in life, we all share the same set of basic human *needs*. Whether you are a stripper at the local gentleman's club, a high school football coach, the President of the United States, a garbage man, or some crotchety old retiree down at the senior citizen home, you are under the direct influence of the six **UNCONSCIOUS PERSONALITY DRIVERS** that affect every human being who has ever lived.

Understanding these forces can now let you become aligned with the **INTERPERSONAL MODALITIES** of the dancer whom you have selected as the focus of your desire. The six basic human needs are:

Comfort

Variety

Significance

Growth

Contribution

Connection

The aforementioned items are the needs that are quietly driving just about every one of our behaviors in some way or another. These are not things that would be gratifying to have or that we want if we can get them. These are needs. We will, consciously *or not*, seek fulfillment of these needs under all circumstances, and at all times **REGARDLESS OF THE CONSEQUENCES**.

Most people seek the satisfaction of the basic human needs perfectly oblivious to the fact that they are doing so and end up causing all sort of serious problems for themselves and the people around them. Complications arising from the subconscious pursuit of the six basic human needs burden pretty much *everybody*.

Both you and the dancer whose attention you covet are uncontrollably affected by the same desire to fulfill these needs at any cost, and understanding this is most relevant especially in the realm of dating. Let's take some time to review these needs, and to consider what they mean in the real world. Always remember that these drives are not simply things you want, things you should do, or things maybe it would be neat to do when you get around to it someday.

The six basic human needs are compulsory and at work within you every moment of every day whether you recognize it or not.

So let's look at each of them in turn:

COMFORT

We want a nice home, a solid relationship, predictable routines, a planned vacation, money in savings and a maxed-out IRA, enough pillows on the bed and a comfy chair to sit in during Monday Night Football.

We want to know that if things get rough out there, we can depend on the stable core of our lives for security and protection. This is what drives us to stay in relationships with people we don't like anymore, work at jobs we hate, and maintain friendships with people from high school that we outgrew years ago.

VARIETY

If the things around us never changed, we would go fucking crazy. We travel to exotic locations, cheat on the people we love, switch jobs, change majors in college, sign up for 500 cable channels when 50 would do just as well, and go shopping for crap we don't need even if we are broke.

One of the reasons that the solitary confinement of criminals is so effective (as well as cruel) is because it deprives inmates of the ability to satisfy this need in even the smallest, most inconsequential ways.

SIGNIFICANCE

In many ways, the need to feel significant is the most fundamental drive of all. We have the absolute need to feel, and to know, that the things we do matter in some way, no matter how small.

Winning awards, getting promoted, being asked for advice or named as an expert in some area, being openly admired for some trait or skill, getting elected, winning fame by acting in films or making music, and getting a sincere card on Father's Day are all examples of significance.

The desires that most of us have to raise successful children who then carry on our legacy are another example of the pursuit of significance. At the end of the day, an entry-level Rolex and a cheap tombstone just aren't enough, we need for our lives to have meant something, and we would all much prefer to find that meaning in our lives while we are still living them.

GROWTH

We have to get better or change in some way otherwise a sense of truly real stagnation sets in. Maybe we go back to school after years in the workforce, learn a new skill, have the opportunity for career advancement, transition from single life to happily married with children, or go from follower to leader.

Our need to become something more than we currently are, to become one day something we never thought possible is as powerful as any of the other needs on this list.

To be denied the opportunity for personal growth and development is tantamount to spiritual murder (or suicide, depending on your perspective.)

People who spend enormous amounts of time and energy advancing their high-level World of Warcraft character to the exclusion of a "normal" social life do so as a means to experience growth when they mistakenly feel it is denied to them in other areas, not because they are antisocial gamer geeks as most people would like to think.

CONTRIBUTION

We all experience the need to contribute, no matter how damn selfish we are. Whether it is picking up the check at dinner, baking cupcakes for the PTA, helping a friend move, mentoring someone, growing our business through our own creativity and dedication, bringing food home for our families, or lending a hand wherever it's needed without being asked doesn't actually matter.

We want what we do to add something positive to the equation; we want to bring something to the table.

The drive to make a connection with others seems almost too obvious to list but don't be deceived by its seeming simplicity. We go to bars, speed date, use online dating services and get high, taking Ecstasy at raves. We have a burning need, each and every one of us, to experience that, *I see you, you see me*, moment of emotional connectedness. No amount of online or distance interactions can replace the spark created by actual **TACTILE CONNECTION**.

Sometimes, just having someone in physical contact with you, whether in a romantic sense or not, is all it takes. Despite wanting something deep, lasting, and meaningful, never forget that we will stop at nothing when it comes to getting our needs met, even if the situations or relationships that provide for what we want are generally negative or harmful to ourselves or the people around us.

So, there you have it, the *Six Basic Human Needs*: **COMFORT, VARIETY, SIGNIFICANCE, GROWTH, CONTRIBUTION AND CONNECTION.** Which of these do you think are most relevant to you? What about to an exotic dancer at your favorite gentleman's club, which does she focus on?

The answer, of course, Is all of the above.

As I said before, these are needs, and we are pursuing them all the time, at any cost, regardless of the consequences whether we are consciously aware of them or not. If you can become focused on these needs in a conscious way, and pay attention to them as they are being expressed by the dancer you are sitting next to, the chances of forming the relationship you seek for will increase by an order of magnitude.

Ignore these needs, and the words and deeds of your intended paramour will sweep around you like the winds of some tropical storm. Yes, it will be a storm of glitter, erratic behavior, all-hours angry text messaging, jealousy and childish outbursts, but it will be a storm nonetheless.

Avoid all that by simply paying attention and knowing that these forces are at work within the object of your desire as surely as they are at work within you. And they are at work within you, make no mistake about that. It is also helpful and pertinent to understand that every problem every person faces stems from the conflicts that arise from the fulfillment of these six needs.

For example, you love your wife and want to stay in the relationship *(comfort)* but cheat on her with some girl you couldn't care less about *(variety)*. This may seem somewhat abstract, so allow me to offer an example of what I am talking about here:

You are interested in a dancer who has a boyfriend with whom she is unhappy. You know this because she is constantly texting him in front of everyone and clearly agitated when doing so. She sometimes may even leave the shift early to go deal with issues at home that relate to her relationship with him.

You know that this dancer likes being a dancer but seems afflicted by some sort of ennui over her career choice. It sometimes seems as if she is growing ever more despondent about her life choices.

She is a student at a local community college but you have been unable to ascertain if there is ever a projected graduation date for her certification or degree. She clearly wants to do something with her life but has no idea what that should be. She is a person whom you might describe as "touchy-feel-y" and seems to have a close relationship with some members of the male club staff.

What follows is *one possible interpretation* of what's going on with this girl:

She is a complete head case with imperfect to horrible taste in men. No matter how awesome any guy turns out to be, she will always prefer somebody who treats her like shit. She likes dancing because it can be an easy way to generate income for someone with no skills, work ethic or sense of personal responsibility but hates it because she still has to work and she thinks that is just too *unfair.*

What she undoubtedly would like is some kind of asshole with lots of money to come along and take care of her for the rest of her life.

She is caught in **THE COMMUNITY COLLEGE TRAP** and under no circumstances will she ever graduate or do anything with the education that she seems so uncommitted to. She has no goals or priorities and does not have the ability to control herself or make any kind of forward progress in life.

She is promiscuous and is probably hitting it with every guy that works at the club, hoping that one of them will be *the one* to rescue her from her crappy boyfriend.

In short, she's a fucking loser, or at least that's one way to look at it. When applying the principles of the *Six Basic Human Needs*, however, that interpretation tends to be radically altered:

Many dancers I have encountered have some sort of abandonment issue and/or some sense that they are alone in the world. We could speculate all day about why that is, but honestly it just doesn't matter, at least for our purposes anyway. This example dancer is sticking around with her jerk of a boyfriend for no other reason than doing so provides a sense of security.

No matter how awful things get between them, there is enough personal history, shared values, memories and latent physical attraction to keep them together and make him her anchor in life. This is the actualization of her need for comfort.

Dancing allows her ability to meet people of the opposite sex under controlled circumstances and to express herself sexually both onstage and off. No matter what she says about it, her life as an adult entertainer provides a level of variety that otherwise could be satisfied only by cheating on her boyfriend.

Somebody who comes from a background of scarcity and neglect, and possesses no real marketable skills or education, may feel that they have nothing worthwhile to offer, nothing that makes them unique. Any guy, however, can tell you that a pretty girl gyrating on their lap in a tiny string bikini is pretty damn memorable and worthwhile to pursue.

Becoming a dancer allows a girl to attain a form of significance that can be hard to argue with in the most jaw-dropping fashion. Just step into any strip joint and see if the women there don't immediately garner your undivided attention.

She is attending college courses not because she has to but because she recognizes that she needs to change in some way. Regardless of how well she performs as a student, the fact that she is getting up in the morning to go attend a lecture after being up all night partying at the club does not indicate that she is some kind of loser failing at her half-ass attempt at scholarship.

Instead, what it actually means is that she has some sort of cognitive awareness of her need for growth and she is willing to make sacrifices for it, even if they are limited in their scope and level of commitment.

Pursuing activities outside of the typical club life, such as going to school, interacting with people and concepts outside of her normal comfort zone allows for additional variety in her life, as well.

Our dancer may be acting as the only real breadwinner in her household, perhaps caring for a child and almost certainly providing for the man-child she thinks of as her boyfriend. It isn't altogether uncommon to find exotic dancers providing for others as well, such as siblings who need a place to stay, aged parents or freeloading friends. This phenomenon is the need for positive contribution directly at work in her life.

While she may be struggling to get the damn bills paid and constantly dodging repo men and debt collectors, she still is acting out on the need to contribute, regardless of her level of success in doing so. The drive for significance is present here too, since being the person who puts food on the table and makes things happen certainly qualifies her role as being one of central importance.

Finally, she often feels isolated and alone. The males in her life have not acted as positive role models, nor have they provided the emotional centering force of comfort and security. The male staff within the club becomes a form of pseudo-family, with the bouncers acting as protective elder brothers, the DJs in the role of favored uncle and the manager holding paternal authority.

This working family provides a sense of connection that is difficult to replicate elsewhere (just like inner city kids joining gangs) and may be the glue that actually holds her life together, providing the energy to face another day.

She seems intimately connected to these people because she is and, while this may manifest in some form of romantic or sexual relationship for some, it is not necessarily so in most cases. You might note also that she is more than likely getting a sense of significance from these relationships since she is *genuinely* relevant to the staff members.

Most likely you can already see how something as straightforward as **RE-FRAMING** this dancer's approach to life can suddenly change who she is to you. Seen through the lens of the basic human needs people become less antagonistic, their motives less murky and suspicious.

Don't get me wrong, the *Example Dancer Girlfriend* above seems like she might be a lot of work to deal with, especially given that she has a boyfriend tracking her phone GPS, but that doesn't mean she is some kind of hopeless loser.

Personally, I wouldn't pursue the hypothetical girl I cited in the example since it would require the investment of too much precious time and effort. That doesn't make her an evil person though, or a slut, or a loser, or any other derogatory appellation you care to assign her. The point of the preceding exercise was simply to open your eyes to the fact that *exotic dancers are genuinely no different from anyone else.*

They go to work, experience issues at home that make demands on their time, carry the same emotional baggage as every other female who has ever lived, worry about the future, stress out over their next birthday, and want to be liked. Just because they are engaged in conversation with you while wearing a sequin-covered gown and eight-inch platform heels changes nothing. The sooner you stop thinking of these girls as objects to be used like tools, pieces of furniture or your new midlife-crisis mobile, the better.

Please don't misunderstand what is being said here, I'm certainly not suggesting that you sit around psychoanalyzing the dancer sitting across the cheap cocktail table from you in a seedy strip joint. There is no point to that, it's a waste of your time and, frankly, you're not qualified to do that anyway.

What I am saying is that being aware of these forces at work within the stripper you have focused on will improve your chances of success dramatically. You will better understand her, and she will feel more comfortable with you.

A woman who is comfortable and secure in the presence of a man becomes open to all sorts of things. And aren't females who are more open to things simply more fun?

TWO

Preparing

CHAPTER 5

Sharp dressed man

SIXTY PERCENT OF THE TIME, IT WORKS EVERY TIME.

- Bill Clinton, Oxford educated Governor of Arkansas and 42nd President; regarded as untrustworthy and morally suspect, was the only person ever tried in congress for getting laid; remains one of the most popular presidents of all time.

While I may not know you personally, I would be willing to bet that, at some point in your life, there has been an occasion which required that you pay particular attention to your appearance.

We all have things that force us to start caring about the clothes we're wearing, like going to church, hiring interviews, funerals, weddings, court appearances, maybe that new *shithole cubicle job* that sucks the life out of you on a daily basis, or whatever. Most of us are accustomed to the idea that there are certain times and places where appropriate dress is desirable, *or even advantageous.*

Perhaps you should consider that heading out for a night at a strip club, with the express intent of attracting a future mate, may be one of those times. It does not matter how you personally feel about **CHURCHING UP** your appearance to go hang with a bunch of strippers, because how you feel about it isn't the point.

Without a doubt, men with enough common sense to pay attention to their own attire, ensuring that their wardrobe can project confidence, affluence, capability and strength will always attract exotic dancers.

If you are willing to spend just a little bit of time and money preparing for your visit to the club, you will almost certainly reap the rewards in the form of greater interest and attention from the dancers you are trying to attract. Women generally pay attention to a man's appearance, using it to gauge his relative social status, habits and *overall suitability as a potential mate.*

Since it doesn't actually take all that much effort to present the proper appearance, this is an area that should always be taken care of prior to meeting up with the girls down at the club. Presenting the proper appearance generally falls into two categories: taking care of personal hygiene issues and ensuring that you always dress for success.

PERSONAL HYGIENE

So, you are heading into a venue where you intend to socialize with members of the opposite sex who are primarily clothed in bare skin, and yet, you have inexplicably decided to come directly to the club from your day job as a landscaper. Your clothes, work stained and wrinkled from a long day's labor, smell like sweat, grass and machine oil. In addition, your clothing is probably more conducive to protecting you from the elements and accidental injury than letting a soft, sweet-smelling woman sit comfortably on your lap.

Seriously, *what the fuck are you thinking?* This is a quick list of things you should take care of before heading down to the club for an **INTIMATE RENDEZVOUS** with your favorite exotic dancer:

Shower, use soap and shampoo

Shave so that she doesn't have to avoid the stubble on your face

Put on fresh clothes

Use deodorant

Brush your teeth, and tongue

Floss and use mouthwash

Lightly apply cologne, avoid using the cheap shit sold in drugstores

Bring breath mints, not gum

Ensure that your pockets are as empty as you can make them

Wear a watch, and leave your cell phone in the car if possible

Leave overly specific jewelry [like a wedding ring] at home

Take a moment to make sure your shoes are clean and serviceable

It is essential that you present the safest, most comfortable, most pleasant presence you possibly can pull off. Making sure you are clean, smell enjoyable without coming off like a French whorehouse, and don't have tons of crap falling out of your pockets is a key part of that. Not having onboard distractions, like a cell phone are another.

After all, are you honestly such a pivotal dude that someone out there is truly going to need to get a hold of you at the club? Why the hell would you want them to anyway?

Removing clues to the reality of your shit-life outside of the club fantasy, like a wedding ring or other identifying items, are yet another. Go in clean, in more ways than one, and you will find that you come out the same way.

DRESS FOR SUCCESS

There's no need to go update your tux (*as if you even have one, you fucking barbarians*) in order to walk into your average strip joint, but unless you like hanging out at total dives frequented by gang members and bikers, I would advise you to dress up a little. It's supposed to be a gentleman's club, a place where men with means and character can meet women who are seeking the same.

Some casual slacks, a well fitted shirt neatly tucked in, a decent belt properly worn, matching socks that cost more than $8 for a 6-pack (*and aren't white*) and real shoes, in good condition, and with a bit of shine on them will do wonders for your appearance.

Note that when I say, shirt I am referring to an actual shirt, one of those things that usually button up the front, have cuffs, and may be worn with a tie. There are many variations on the basic shirt concept, often worn without a tie, that convey the correct image anyway, such as the iconic Indiana Jones **ADVENTURE STYLE**, or modern **SAFARI SHIRTS**. Polo shirts also qualify, if you're into golf or, you know....polo (ah, but who truly has time for polo these days, know what I mean?)

T-shirts, however, do not qualify. T-shirts, properly speaking, are underwear. As in they are meant to be worn under an actual shirt. I don't care how incredible the trendy "all-over" tribal design is or how much it cost you to purchase from Ed Hardy or the Affliction store, a t-shirt is fucking underwear, and you look like an idiot walking around in an intimate, social situation wearing one.

Well, you'd look ridiculous unless you've been invited to a pajama party at the **PLAYBOY MANSION**, in which case wearing your underwear might be ok but since you're *actually at a pajama party* I recommend wearing actual pajamas.

You're all a bunch of fucking savages, you know that?

I also highly recommend owning and wearing, **A JACKET**. A so-called **SPORTS COAT**, in its own way, is perfect for this kind of thing, but any decent, matching **BLAZER** will do. If you like, you can always wear it into the club and then remove it at your table.

A jacket hanging off the back of your club chair allows the dancers to see that you have a little more going on and take shit more seriously than the asshole at the bar in shorts, flip-flops and a backwards ball cap.

A jacket can also make a handy place for storing extra junk from your pants pockets when you head back to get dances. Put your extra shit in the jacket pockets, and take it with you to the **VIP ROOM**.

You can drape it across the dance area furniture that you are using so that nothing goes missing, while simultaneously not having your *car keys ground painfully into your thigh* every time the stripper puts her weight on you.

Ties are optional, and may make you look a little too dressed up. No need to make yourself unapproachable by accident. Also, a tie can serve as a target for drunken strippers who think that yanking you around by the tie is both fun and endearing. Having a tie knotted around your neck may be a handicap should you accidentally find yourself in some kind of parking lot brawl, bar fight or other altercation. I suggest avoiding those kinds of situations irrespective of *whether you wear a tie or not.*

If you do decide to go with a tie, or your outfit just doesn't look right without one, loosen up the collar. Don't pull the tie askew as if to suggest that your day at the insurance brokerage just kicked your ass sideways, and you can't breathe from all the fucking excitement. Instead, artfully loosen up the tie as if you think you're **MICHAEL BUBLÈ** about to hit the stage in Vegas or something.

And then there are shoes. If you have to scrimp on the cost and quality of your wardrobe due to financial constraints, shoes are the one place you should clearly make an exception. The quality, perceived cost, wear and condition of a person's shoes say a lot about what kind of person they are, and this is something that most women are somehow directly jacked into.

If you look and feel fantastic, but your shoes are crap or are falling to pieces, any woman with half a brain in her head will make a mental note that you are full of shit, even if she doesn't actually call you out on it.

Your shoes don't have to be some ridiculously expensive set of Italian loafers, but they shouldn't be picked up from your local discount retailer for $15 either. Even if you, for some reason don't care what other people think, I promise you that shelling out a minimum $100 for **A DECENT SET OF KICKS** will make you a happier, more confident person.

The extra effort required to make sure that you look, smell and feel fantastic when you come in physical contact with soft, half-naked women is worth the relatively small amount of time and money that you'll have to invest. Shop around for the stuff you wear, balancing quality with cost, avoiding the standard reliance on big-box retailers for your wardrobe.

Try, whenever you can, to have things **TAILORED**. If money is an issue, check your local dry cleaner for cheap tailoring services. It won't be as slick or comprehensive as you would get at a men's clothier or tailor, but they can usually make sure your clothes are *the right length, and the waistlines fit correctly.* Most guys don't think of it much, but the accuracy of a hemline or fit of the pant waist can often make a **DRAMATIC** difference in a man's appearance.

This is another helpful hint: place a mirror near the front door of your house or apartment. Get in the habit of checking yourself before walking out the door. Being forced to stare at yourself for a moment before going out in public can help you catch any issues with your appearance, as well as giving you the opportunity to practice looking good, standing tall, and projecting a confident persona.

Remember that how you look makes a statement about who you are; so take the time and effort to be a man that any stripper you meet will be attracted to.

Oh, and quit biting your fingernails, you *savages*.

CHAPTER 6

Love machine

I'M IN LOVE WITH A STRIPPER.

- Thomas Otway, author of the 1681 comedy, "The Soldier's Fortune" in which the term stripping was first used in reference to a woman taking her clothes off for money.

Despite some of the things I have said so far, I truly do like strippers, quite a bit, in fact.

That's why I would hate to think that some kind of misogynistic dick might be reading this book, thinking he's gonna lay down all sorts of heinous crap with what he may learn from me. It's particularly fucked when you stop to consider that he'd be pulling his shit on some unsuspecting girl probably sitting beside him dressed in nothing more than her underwear and a smile.

Growing up without their dads and not knowing what to do about it is the only crime most strippers are actually guilty of, thus becoming the target of some man-boy's asinine crap fetish is something both *undeserved and wholly unfair.*

So, let's clarify if we can. If you hate dancers, or women in general, please stop reading this book and go back to *torturing puppies, training to be a cage fighter, voting Republican* or whatever it is that you do with your time.

Gentlemen's clubs are places you go to revel in the experience of intimately connecting with members of the opposite sex in a liberated, erotic, social environment. It's like a church where you worship the idea of being with an *idealized version* of **FEMININE SEXUALITY**.

If you don't like, or can't accept the idea of strip joint as a form of **SEXUAL TEMPLE**, don't worry about it. Instead, just think of it as a miniature theme park that allows you to forget the oft-depressing truth of your 9 to 5 life and, for a moment, touch, taste, smell, hear and see all that you have been missing. This, by the way, is a *lot*.

ENVY

In this context, the correctly created strip club experience generates envy, and that is a marvelous thing. When I say envy I mean it as a distinct and separate emotional experience from jealousy. **ENVY** is a *positive emotion* in moderation, whereas jealousy is always negative, regardless of what women's magazines may be saying these days.

Envy is the emotional impulse that arises when we see something that we don't currently possess, and feel a powerful desire to have it for ourselves. This urge is often coupled with the realization that we may have this thing if we want, and if we're willing to do the work required to get it. **JEALOUSY,** on the other hand, is that nasty thing that springs from fear of loss when we discover our wife or girlfriend **SEXTING** with some other guy.

You and I should always be willing to accept the intrusion of envy into the crap routine that normally passes for our lives.

The deep, underlying force of an emotion such as this stands as a reminder that **LAZINESS AND PROCRASTINATION** are nothing more than a way of *excusing the current, unfulfilling life conditions we may be willing to tolerate.*

Envy can be the cause of finally getting back to the gym and losing the weight you always planned to, changing the way you dress, switching jobs, altering spending patterns, putting some money in your savings, setting goals, going back to school, etc.

HATERS

Strip clubs are the ultimate temple to the powerful mental states of envy, desire, sexual arousal, and **ESCAPIST FANTASY**. Somebody walking into one of these places with the need to denigrate women, using terms like *whore, slut, cunt,* or openly referring to the females as *bitches* has an evident problem. If, by some chance, you are one of these guys...*and yes, I know you're not, but still*...I suggest that you pick up the phone and find yourself a **THERAPIST**.

Honestly though, it's not just the dancers who are victimized by such vulgar displays of *he-man-girl-hating* in the strip club either. Most of the male clientele aren't there because they want to make asses of themselves, feel stupid, worthless, and unattractive or because they want other people to feel that way.

Most guys are coming into the club because they're **LONELY** and they need someone to talk to. Maybe their wife is a cold shrew and a young, soft girl wriggling around in their laps is about the best they can hope for in life, how do you know?

Hating on the strippers and acting like an **ASS-HAT** blows the experience for the other customers, guys who are just looking for a little relief from their **SHIT-LIVES**.

Negative assholes, the guys who are genuinely just **HATERS**, generally don't last long in the club anyway. Haters usually show their true colors sooner rather than later and get the heave-ho from the premises. Sometimes it's starting fights, arguing or insulting the staff, refusing to pay for dances, trying to skip on a bar tab or flicking quarters at the girl on stage.

Whatever the issue is, they aren't welcome for terribly long, yet some haters have a cunning ability to stick around even when they're clearly not welcome. Hopefully, the club you hang around at doesn't tolerate their form of bullshit much.

SUCKERS

The misogynistic dancer haters are generally at one end of the customer spectrum, but who is at the other end? At the other end, both literally and figuratively, is a guy who is fully engaged in being a gullible, mouth-breathing stripper-slave. This guy is truly a sucker for stripper-game, and can't seem to keep things straight. **SUCKERS** are *true believers* in wonder and beauty of the dancer that they're into this week.

A sucker thinks of his stripper as a thoroughly lovely person who honestly just needs some help navigating this wicked world of ours, and he is just determined, for the moment, to be her knight in shining armor. Except that it never works out that way, not really.

The sucker worldview does not admit to *real human flaws in the real human dancers*. They do not, or perhaps cannot, conceive of a 23 year old topless showgirl as being someone who would be **SELFISH, DUMB, INEXPERIENCED, OR PETTY.**

Anything that a stripper does "wrong" is explained as outside circumstances acting in a way that just can't be controlled. In other words, true suckers mirror the emotional states and worldviews of the young dancers that they are so enamored with, at least when they are in the context of the club. Maybe when these guys are at home alone they stop to reflect on things and soberly recognize that the girls are flawed beings full of their own bullshit...yeah, *probably not.*

It has been my experience that most of these guys are true believers pretty much twenty-four hours a day, seven days a week. When some girl finally disappoints them for the hundredth time, and they just can't take it anymore, they simply switch the focus of their affection to some other dancer.

Despite any individual setbacks, however, the Sucker belief in the sanctity of the dancer remains generally unshaken, even if they are now forced to shun an individual girl or two who just couldn't recognize the Sucker for the glittering cavalier that he believes himself to be.

Suckers are the type of guys who are sitting down to dinner with their family when their **ATF** (All Time Favorite) dancer secretly texts their phone with a message like,

"Get your ass down to the club right now or I will never speak to you again!"

Now, just between you and me, the idea that this dancer is never, ever going to call our guy again is quite ludicrous. Even if she did follow through on her threat it could likely be the *best thing* that could happen to this customer.

Because...Well, because she's a fucking asshole and, if nothing else, deserves to get her ass *blown off* by this guy.

Nonetheless, our sucker is probably going to freak the fuck out, thinking that his darling dancer girl is truly mad at him for *really-real*. He thinks that she deserves the best and that he has simply let his girl down, just like every other man in her life. He's not one of them, is he? A follow-up message from his dominating stripper crush might read,

"You know that my rent is due tomorrow, how can you be so fucking irresponsible?"

In this case, our man would undoubtedly offer an excuse for leaving the dinner table, claiming some forgotten errand requiring a trip to the store before it closes for the night. While he may actually end up going to a store on his way to the club, it will be just to pick up some extra cash at the ATM, and some flowers for the stripper he has so thoroughly disappointed.

Dancers treat haters and suckers with practically opposite amounts of contempt, disgust, appreciation and respect. Haters normally get the respect of the dancers (if not the love), after all, they are seemingly unaffected by stripper game and are utterly unpredictable in temperament and action.

In many ways, this kind of guy can remind the girls of their abusive step dad or loser boyfriend and, in its way that can be attractive. Haters also get the disgust because they are assholes who, as I said, remind these vulnerable, psychologically scarred girls of their abusive step dads and loser boyfriends.

Suckers tend to pick up the reverse end on the emotional scale here. Suckers are treated, at least behind their backs, with total contempt mainly because no self-respecting attractive female can seriously think of a guy so easily henpecked and controlled as truly being a man. On the other hand, suckers are genuinely appreciated for what they are: a walking ATM that come when called.

The hater and the sucker may represent extreme ends of the strip club customer scale, but there are certainly plenty of other customer types that lay in the gulf between them.

These two kinds of club denizens are not necessarily indicative of the kind of guy that patronizes clubs, hangs out with strippers or gets lap dances at a **BACHELOR PARTY**. They are simply highly visible and recognizable extremes.

CUSTOMERS

I should probably take a moment to explain the difference between the terms customer, and guest or visitor. For our purposes, a **GUEST OR VISITOR** will be a somewhat casual patron at the club, or perhaps someone who may stop in one time, never to be seen at the club again.

This is typically someone who has walked into the club just looking to have an enjoyable time while they are there. They aren't planning to make a career out of it, get to know anyone on a personal level, or even come back necessarily.

This would include bachelor parties, groups of guys out partying or anybody who just dropped by for fun or because their wife or girlfriend is out of town and they think they can get away with it. Guests who are just visiting the club on a whim aren't in the running to catch one of the girls in a moment of weakness and score some ass.

Those of you who fit into this category and still believe or tell your friends that you can hit it with the girls at the local club are wrong. Actually, *lying to yourself* and otherwise looking like a complete juvenile asshole is probably more a far more accurate way to say that.

Strippers don't get excited by three drunken jerks too scared to be in a strip club by themselves. Your attempt to make it rain on stage with a handful of sweaty dollar bills may certainly have been breathtaking, but you still aren't getting laid in the VIP room tonight.

A **CUSTOMER**, on the other hand, is somebody who makes regular, often predictable appearances at the club. These people will normally schedule their appearance in the club to coincide with the presence of one or more girls in whom they are interested.

The objects of the visits are most likely specific dancers but could also be a favorite waitress or bartender. Usually one or more people on staff, as well as strippers they tend to favor, will have the customer's phone number and be familiar enough with this person that they can openly send them text messages urging them to come in.

To have any real chance of making a connection with an exotic entertainer, you will almost assuredly need to be a

CUSTOMER, well known and approachable. The trick is that you must become the right kind of customer and then know how to exploit that status to your benefit. This is one of the reasons why you'll need to understand who the various customer types are and where you are going to fit within the strip club ecosystem.

REAL LIFE

So, perhaps being a hater is a poor choice for the man looking to form an outside relationship with an exotic dancer. Hopefully you know also that being a dick in real life is probably not a winning option either.

While I will leave that up to you to decide, try to keep in mind that acting like a douchebag toward the clerk at 7–11 may not be any more conducive to *positive and fulfilling life outcomes* than acting abusive toward a twenty-something stripper is.

A brief note here on things that are in real life and the distinction between those things and what happens in the club environment. Inside a strip joint, once you pay your cover and pass the doorman, assaulted by loud music, quite often lubricated by alcohol, and inundated with attractive people of the opposite sex waltzing around in string bikinis you must realize that you <u>have</u> a made a departure from that which is strictly real.

What is happening here is nothing short of a middle-age crisis daydream fantasy writ large. **REALITY,** that thing that normally involves paying bills, schlepping off to a job you fucking hate, calling your mom on her birthday, taking the kids to the dentist, and mowing your lawn *does not apply here*. So leave it at the door. Similarly, the things that happen within the confines of the club have no business existing outside it.

You need to make this distinction and create a useful separation that allows you to enjoy the fantasy of the club and pursue your **HOOKER WITH A HEART OF GOLD** dream girl while doing so in a way that does not impair, impact or damage things that exist in real life. Take a moment to recall, if you will, that the most notable things outside the club are *almost always people*.

Wives, girlfriends, kids, other family members, those you work for or whom work for you. So make the distinction between what's real and what's a fantasy; draw a line and be careful how and when you cross it, and with whom. You'll be happier that way, trust me.

FALLING FOR GAME

Honestly there is nothing wrong in absolute terms with being a guy who is always at the mercy of **STRIPPER GAME**. Almost all of those guys are getting something out of being a sucker; otherwise they wouldn't be doing it. Precisely what they are taking from the experience varies considerably from one customer to another, may change over time and is entirely subjective.

Despite how hard it may be to determine what positive benefit a sucker is reaping from his arrangement with a dancer, know that he is getting *something* that he desires, and whatever that may be is making him happy, even if it looks goofy to you.

As I've noted before, however, being on this status within a gentlemen's club is unlikely to make you seem like a solid choice as a mate. The girls might fight with each other for your attention, which is certainly gratifying if you are ignored at home, but that is just a function of the fact that you will be a solid, easily controlled customer once acquired.

Dancers are territorial about their money customers and will fight to keep them. They also may be willing to meet with you outside the club for what is known as **MONEY DATES**.

We'll touch on the idea of money dates a little later. For the moment, just know that they exist, they don't *necessarily* involve sex, and that if your intended target dancer is going out on these things with another customer it does not mean that she is a lost cause and that you are out of the running. On the other hand, if the girl you are after does go out on these things with customers, it has the potential to cause problems and is something I'd be wary of.

Suckers would like to think that outside social engagements like the money date provide some level of legitimacy for their relationship with the dancer in question. They often believe that this is an indication that he is dating the stripper who happens to be walking around with him at the mall or wherever.

Here, we are confronted with another problem endemic to sucker status; a false belief that he is involved in an, as yet, unconsummated serious relationship. I have seen these guys get super upset when their "girlfriend" goes off doing something stupid or ignores them for another customer altogether. *Do not be this guy.*

LOVE, LUST AND CREATIVE NAMING

By now you are most likely wondering what kind of customer you'll need to be in order to attain success with the dancers. Well, other than just mainly being authentic, fun, and respectful, you should be, and probably are, **ADDICTED TO STRIPPERS** to some extent.

Why else would you even be reading this book right now, if you weren't somehow stuck on the idea of taking one of the girls you see at the club, and making her your own? You should just be honest with yourself, admit that you are addicted to strippers and are seeking a way to make your dream of romantically connecting with them a reality.

Do you know what the difference between the early stages of fixated, physically-based sexual attraction (commonly referred to as **LUST**) and addictive behavior is? If you aren't sure of the answer, don't sweat it, the scientific and medical communities don't know for sure either. Fact is, the same things happen to you emotionally, mentally and physiologically whether you are lusting after some new person in your life or heading to your dealer to pick up an **EIGHT BALL OF COKE**.

There are definite chemical processes that occur when you become seriously attracted to someone, normally involving something known as the **LOVE MOLECULE**. As you can see, the imagination of world science in creative naming has outdone itself here. Way to go the extra mile on *that one*, science dudes.

Be that as it may, this so-called Love Molecule works literally to addict you to the physical presence of the person you have fallen in lust with. That is why it actually physically hurts when she's not around. Turns out you aren't the emotional man-girl you thought you were, or at least *not so much*. The effect of this thing wears off after about a year or so and, in good relationships, is replaced with high production of the hormone *Oxytocin*, known as the **CUDDLE HORMONE**.

And yes, Science just scored another point in the category of: "Giving overly obvious names to shit that we probably could have figured out for ourselves."

The Love Molecule ensures the continuation of the species by forcing you to want to break down any barrier, overcome any obstacle and risk *everything* for a chance to bang it out with someone of the opposite sex.

The Cuddle Hormone then ensures that you successfully pair-bond with that person, and team up to raise your offspring, hopefully protecting them from dangerous predators, like **WOLVES, ZOMBIES AND THE RAMPAGING ORCS OF MIDDLE-EARTH.**

LOVERS

Apparently, there is little difference, scientifically speaking, between someone hopelessly addicted, and someone deeply, lustfully, in love. So, instead of worrying about whether you're barking up the wrong tree or obsessing over something unhealthy, you should seek simply to embrace what you love. If what you love is strippers, then embrace that and become **THE LOVER.**

For the true lover of anything, exotic dancers included, the pleasure derived from their vice most often lies in the pursuit of it. Satisfying such a desire may lead to actual, permanent, healthy fulfillment. Of course, it can just as often lead to a continuation of the pursuit in other venues, with other targets or for higher stakes. Such is the risk one takes when seeking out something as inherently unstable and dangerous as forming ongoing, intimate relationships with strippers.

If you have somehow, in whatever way, become fixated on exotic dancers, then what you need most is the ability to actualize your desire in the most positive way possible.

There is no need to stress out about it if this is what you're into since chasing love with the girls down at the local strip joint is far more enjoyable than a lot of other things you might do with your life. Embrace your desire, *seek mastery* over your impulse driven behaviors, and learn to remove the futility and frustration from your interactions with the women you love.

I'm not using the word, **LOVE** lightly either. That's one of the funny things about stripper addiction; those afflicted with it genuinely love strippers for what they truly are. They are sexual, independent women with real issues that can suddenly cause their therapists to disappear for weeks on end to some remote Vermont meditation retreat.

Exotic dancers alternate between being the best and worst that womanhood can offer, and have the ability not only to draw the greatness within a man forth but also to induce extreme recklessness and **SUICIDAL BEHAVIOR**.

A lover of these women truly appreciates them inside the club and out, by the name they use on stage, and the one they were given at birth, whether in heels and a thong or pajama bottoms and t-shirt.

Someone like this always tries to keep enough perspective on the situation to know that this may not be appropriate and, most likely, will not end well. Yet, this may be the greatest weapon that can be brought to bear in their pursuit of the **ULTIMATE GIRLFRIEND**; the ability to see strippers as women first.

Perhaps real lovers may be the only type of customer patronizing clubs that retains this ability. Mostly, other people tend to see the girls as a stripper first, only belatedly realizing that dancers are actual people with all the same issues as other women, if not more. You can be sure that this can be *somewhat disappointing* for the average guy who just scored his first round of dancer ass and is now confronted with her reality the morning after.

If you actually can love strippers though, you'll generally avoid that kind of perceptual delusion. The women you are chasing are those who have fully decided to possess and inhabit their sexual selves on a near full time basis as a means to an income and an identity, but that doesn't define who they are as people. You'll always need to relate first to the woman as a person, and then to her choice of identity. Not only will this be more compelling for you, but for the strippers that become the **FOCUS** of your attention, as well.

I think that it bears repeating that the dancers who work in adult show clubs are typically seen as strippers first and often as nothing more than that by most guys who come into the club. Thus, they become empty vessels for whatever emotional baggage, odd aspirations or perverted desires that the customers wish to pour into them. They are never real people themselves with their own lives fully in progress.

Remember to **REFRAME** your encounters with at the club so that you can see the stripper first as being a woman, then as a woman being an exotic dancer whether out of financial need or as some form of lifestyle choice. Being a stripper is just something that your girl *does*, not necessarily what she is. If you can do this, the actual physiological change in the way you interact with your girl will make a real difference in how you both view each other.

If you do love dancers, and have the **DESIRE** and free time to date them, then there is no reason in the world why you can't succeed. Strippers are people too, you know, and tend to have the same sets of needs, dreams and desires as anyone else you might meet. What sets them apart is that they live in a world in which being used for one's physical appearance, and *presumption* of **PROMISCUITY** is commonplace.

In other words, **THEY KNOW THAT YOU JUST WANT TO FUCK THEM**. Or they think they do. Getting around that barrier is one of the primary things this book is about. If you can do that, you may just find that dating exotic dancers is one of the easiest things you ever done.

The hard part is living with them afterwards.

CHAPTER 7

Jackass

I CAME HERE TO KICK ASS AND CHEW BUBBLEGUM...AND I'M ALL OUTTA BUBBLEGUM.

- Theodore Roosevelt, Secretary of the Navy, commander of the Rough Riders, 26th President of the United States, inventor of manliness and getting shit done.

When you are in a strip club, pursuing that dancer that you have fixated on, you may encounter a series of potential challenges to avoid or master. I would like us to take a just a few moments to run through and clarify some of these things, so that when you do run up against them, you *will* be prepared.

 It's better rehashing things a few extra times, even obvious things, than to be left with a stupid look on your face or lacking the right thing to say.

ASKING FOR SEX

I think we've already mentioned the deal about asking girls to go home with you. This is a no-no and nothing happy will come from it, *for you at least*. Some dancers will get their teeny, tiny panties all in a bunch over a proposition like that. Some may even decide to involve the security staff and/or the club manager.

This could be a fantastic way for you to get your ass kicked out of the club, possibly even **86'D** (permanently banned) from the club itself. Since any girl that would actually agree to such a thing isn't truly going to be worth the time, *why bother?*

FAKE JOB OFFERS

This is equally true for propositions that seem more innocent, yet are simply a less direct way of asking the same thing. An example of this would be asking a girl to be the bartender (or something to that effect) at your weekly poker game. Offering some totally bullshit job, like that of **PERSONAL ASSISTANT**, that mainly involves her hanging out with you also falls into this realm.

This kind of thinly-veiled sham is, in its own way, worse than simply asking her to go to a motel and give you head. A straight up **SEXUAL PROPOSITION** at least involves a certain amount of honesty, whereas this kind of thing taints you as a dirty *creeper* without even enough balls to ask openly.

PRIVATE PARTIES

If you legitimately need a stripper as the centerpiece entertainment at your best friend's bachelor party next week, your local strip club probably isn't the best place to look despite what you might think. The type of entertainer that is available for **PRIVATE ENGAGEMENTS** like a bachelor party is totally different from the average girl you will find down at the club.

There are plenty of services online and in the phone book that are specifically equipped to handle private party requests, but remarkably few of the people involved in that kind of thing also work in strip clubs.

BOYFRIENDS

What possible motive could you have for asking about her boyfriend? Yet, over and over again, customers in the club seem to think that finding this out is somehow of utmost importance. It's not. In fact, asking about her **BOYFRIEND** only serves to remind the girl you are talking to that the fantasy she may be enjoying with you inside the club is not actually real and that her true life and love is probably sitting at home playing video games and watching their kid or something. How can you drawing attention to the man she shares a bed with every night *possibly* help you, or your cause?

If a woman wants to have sex with you, she will do so despite any putative relationship status. Any answer you get from a dancer will be a lie anyway, no matter what the truth is. Whether or not he actually exists, there is nothing served by inquiring after the boyfriend, so just don't do it, *ever*.

TALKING ABOUT YOUR BAGGAGE

This should be so obvious as to go without saying, but guys do it time and time again, so it must not be as obvious as I think it is. Do not, *under any circumstance*, talk about your shitty existing relationship, your ex-wife, the kids or any of that nonsense. Remember how we earlier mentioned the division between things that exist *in real life* and things that exist strictly inside the club? Well, here is a perfect example of that.

You are inside the club right now, and all that other crap that loads you down on a daily basis doesn't exist here. There is no way that the girl in the thigh-high stockings and push-up bra sitting next to you needs to hear about the amount of alimony you are paying, or the most recent fight with that bitch girlfriend of yours. Not only does she not need to hear about it, but she honestly doesn't want to.

On one hand, talking about that kind of stuff detracts from the amount of attention you are paying to her. Doing so can make you appear to be distracted by the mundane life you've chosen to accept, and to her, those things will seem more significant to you than the time you have to spend with her. Further, going into detail about visits from the in-laws, or admitting that your wife forced you to buy a minivan when what you actually wanted was a Camaro will only serve to lower your **SOCIAL VALUE** in her eyes.

LYING YOUR ASS OFF

Seriously, there is no point to this, yet people do it all the time. Now you are saying, "But wait, you just said not to talk about my real life..." Yes, I did say that. Don't talk about your real life. If the details of your real life were fascinating, you would be out **BANGING SUPERMODELS** every night instead of lurking around strip joints. Your real life is boring, encumbered by all sorts of baggage, and has a tendency to *lower your social value* in the estimation of your **PROSPECTIVE STRIPPER GIRLFRIEND.**

That doesn't mean you should be lying to her though. If the point of this whole exercise is to take your relationship with her to the next level, then I promise you that, at some point, your lies will be found out. Why bother with lies and all the work that they entail to maintain?

I said *don't talk about* your dumb crap, but that does not require you to replace it with even stupider lies. Simply don't talk about it. Instead, focus on her, and focus on the experience you share with her in your **FANTASY** club environment.

If you're downright ballsy, you could always **ROLE-PLAY** some kind of fantasy relationship that exists only during the times in which you are in each other's presence inside the club. You'll need her permission and active cooperation for that, of course. I guarantee, however, that she will find something of that nature far more entertaining than most other things you do.

Plus, if you get proficient at pretending an actual relationship with her, you might just find that one day it stops being play acting and starts being something real. Girls are like that, especially the faded and **BROKEN PRINCESSES** that most strippers truly are inside their hearts.

BRINGING SAND TO THE BEACH

In the unlikely event that you are unfamiliar with the above saying, it means that bringing something into a situation where that thing already exists in abundance is redundant in the extreme. Bringing chicks with you to a strip clubs is just one of those things.

Not only does it not make a whole lot of sense wasting your time dragging some girl with you to the club, but it clearly will divert your time and attention *from the dancer that you are supposedly pursuing*. Since the dancer will be aware of this, it will do little for your relationship except perhaps stall or kill it as she gets pissed off at your idiotic insensitivity.

In addition, while we might not think of it consciously, gentlemen's clubs are called that for a reason, and it's not that the patrons are necessarily all **GENTLEMEN**. Strip joints are a place for men to go and enjoy the company of barely clothed female entertainers. Somehow, guys grow up with a basic understanding of strip clubs and how they work. I'm not sure if it's encoded in our **DNA** or simply passed along socially, although if I had to guess I would say that it's *both* actually.

Females in our society do not have the same **BIOLOGICAL HARD WIRING** and **SOCIAL CONDITIONING**. Hence, females in a strip club rarely understand basic etiquette or behavioral rules that men take for granted. They don't know what their role or purpose is in an environment like that, so they act out, usually in a *negative* way. They compete, act jealous, purposely divert attention from the dancers who are working, mistakenly believe that they must somehow "out-stripper" the strippers, and become catty bitches that get you thrown out on your ass.

A lot of people will try to convince you that bringing girls is a *brilliant* idea, since it proves to the dancers that you are a safe guy that can pull chicks, thus more attractive than the average dude that shows up to the club **STAG**. While this may work quite well in other social situations, like an ultra-lounge or a party, the people who tell you to pull this move in a strip club *have no fucking idea* what they are talking about.

BRINGING SAND TO THE BEACH, PART 2: THE REVERSE

There is one sort of situation in which bringing sand to the beach will work out in your favor, so let's discuss it. If you have a female friend that *honestly* holds you in high regard is not a romantic competitor, doesn't mind a night out at a strip club, will positively stay on her *best* behavior at all times, is down to be your wing man for the night, and truly wants to see you succeed, then by all means go ahead and bring her.

This can't be some kind of spontaneous, "Hey, let's go hit the strip club," kind of moment...it must be preplanned and scripted. She has to understand that *she is playing a role* intended to result in getting you laid at some point with the stripper of your choice.

She has to understand the purpose of her presence, and be willing and able to play the role to the hilt. This outing with your wing-girl is not about fun or her having a terrific time, it's about furthering **YOUR AGENDA** with the chick in the school girl costume, and your gal-pal genuinely has to get that through her head and be enthusiastic about playing her part.

But what is her part? Is it to pretend to be a girl you're screwing to create jealousy within your intended stripper target? No, nothing as stupid as that, and remember what we said earlier about lying? Yeah, that's right, why bother? Your chick friend's role is *to be honest*.

You are her friend, and she thinks you are some kind of **MAGNIFICENT FUCKING BASTARD**. She is *so* glad that you bothered to bring her out to the club with you tonight. You and her boyfriend (fiancé, husband, whatever) are devoted friends, and you are the *only* person he trusts to guard his lover out at a strip joint.

Your chick friend should be pouring honey into the dancer's ear on your behalf. Not going overboard, just letting a few positive things slip her and there that work to establish **SAFETY, SECURITY AND SOCIAL VALUE** in the heart of the object of your desire. Be wary though, this kind of thing can easily be overdone and, if not pulled off correctly, could end up doing more harm than good. Still, it is the exception to the rule, and if done well, *can* advance your cause immeasurably.

DRUGS

Fucking *don't*. Don't come into the club all jacked up on crap, don't come in rolling balls and wanting to touch everyone, don't come in smelling like you just hot boxed your car on the way in. Don't ask a dancer to score drugs for you since it implies that she looks like someone who does, buys or sells drugs, and most women, strippers included, will *hardly* consider that a compliment.

Plus, what are you, some kind of cop? I guarantee that, within minutes of you asking her for shit, the word to stay away from the **NARC** at the corner table (that's *you*) will get around to everyone in the club. Don't offer to sell either, since it has all the same connotations, you maybe being an undercover cop included.

And really, if you *are* selling in a strip club, then your purpose for being there is clearly your own personal, **ECONOMIC AGENDA**, *not* because you are interested in the stripper you claim to be pursuing. Your **PARAMOUR** will pick up on that, and that awareness will *surely* torpedo all the hard work you've been doing to connect with her.

An additional down side of all this is that dealing drugs inside a strip club, you are placing the legal and economic well-being of *the entire staff and all the dancers* at risk. Those people have food to put on the table, and your **ZANY HIJINKS** vis-à-vis slanging shit in their club *might not* be perceived in a positive way. The club environment might rapidly go from warm and sunny to cold and inhospitable in the blink of an eye.

Finding yourself in the alley behind the club with a bouncer cracked out on **STEROIDS AND ADDERALL** who thinks you're trying to take food out of the mouth of his six-month old daughter becomes a definite possibility.

KEEPING YOUR HANDS TO YOURSELF

I'll keep this one short, since it really, *seriously* shouldn't require that much of an explanation. A true gentleman doesn't kiss and tell; neither does he grope, pinch, or try to slide a finger into a girl's vagina.

When a dancer bends over in front of him during a private dance, he doesn't lean forward and stick his face between her cheeks. Do that kind of shit with her once you have her home, and you're both in the mood to party.

Don't ask her to lean in so you can whisper something to her, then flip the script and go for a kiss instead. That is some downright creepy molester business; if you want to get anywhere with the girls, putting out serious rape vibes is not the way to do it.

Don't run your hands all over her body if she is sitting with you, don't try to "accidentally" pull her bikini aside, don't pull or tug on the straps or ties hoping for a wardrobe malfunction, don't forcibly hold her in your lap by gripping her hips.

Absolutely do not, under any circumstances, touch her, or attempt to touch her with any item or body part containing, covered in, dripping or actively secreting any bodily fluids; saliva and semen in particular.

Finally, don't whip it out *ever*, under *any* circumstances. I know that there are situations in which emotions run high and your body responds in natural and predictable ways. I know that your stripper girl genuinely *seems* to like the way you are responding to her. I know she truly, really seems to want it. Maybe she even whispered some shit in your ear about how much she'd like to see it, to touch it or...*whatever.*

Do not take your dick out in public and wave it around at people. In case you are unclear on this, the entire interior space of every strip joint in America is considered *in public*.

When I worked in clubs, we would catch guys pulling their shit out all the time. We would always respond by shining our flashlights on them, preventing them from zipping up, then marching them the long way through the club, before pushing them out into the parking lot.

Yeah...I'm thinking that it's better if you don't take your dick out in public

CHAPTER 8

House rules

ALL YOU HAVE TO DO IS FOLLOW THREE SIMPLE RULES. ONE, NEVER UNDERESTIMATE YOUR OPPONENT. EXPECT THE UNEXPECTED. TWO TAKE IT OUTSIDE. NEVER START ANYTHING INSIDE THE BAR UNLESS IT'S ABSOLUTELY NECESSARY. AND THREE, BE NICE.

-Dalton's Law, as conceived by English chemist, meteorologist and physicist John Dalton as he moonlighted as a bouncer at the infamous "Double Deuce" night club in 1801.

You might as well know that there are certain conventions, **EXPECTATIONS**, and generally socialized understandings to live by when hanging out down at the local *Billy-Bob's Beaver Emporium*, or wherever the fuck it is that you like to go.

Just like any other social activity that people engage in, there are ways by which shit *just gets done*, and if you don't respect the time-honored methodology, you risk being **SHUNNED, BANNED, AND OR GETTING YOUR ASS KICKED.**

So, without further ado, here are the rules:

Don't show up drunk, high or otherwise intoxicated.

Bring your id.

Don't bring weapons with you into the club.

If you are bringing weapons into the club, make sure somebody else carries them for you.

Don't bitch about being carded or searched.

Bring enough cash to pay the door charge at minimum.

If you earn the right to free entry, you won't have to ask, so don't bother asking.

Always smile and tip.

Never talk shit to the bouncers.

Don't act disrespectful to any female in the club.

Don't try to disrobe dancers against their will by yanking on or pulling aside their costumes.

If you have to vomit, get your ass to the bathroom.

If you drink a lot, know where the bathroom is.

Don't piss yourself because you didn't want to interrupt the dance.

Don't hit anyone, except in self-defense.

Avoiding your opponent's head and neck in a fight prevents lawsuits and jail time.

Don't use weapons (broken bottles, pool cues) unless it's the only way to save your own life.

Don't call the cops unless it's the only way to save lives.

Don't ask club employees or dancers to call the cops unless it's the only way to save lives.

Don't ever threaten to call the cops as a way of intimidating club employees or dancers.

Don't make threats you aren't prepared to back up with immediate and decisive action.

Remember to smile and tip.

Don't climb on to the stage.

If you do climb on stage, and you're told to get down, do it right away.

Don't put your feet up on, climb on, or stand on the furniture...it's not your fucking house.

Don't argue your tab for dances, just pay it. If they cheated you, don't go back.

Always settle your tab at the bar before you leave.

If you had a tab at the bar, make sure you get your credit card and id back.

Call a cab if you're drunk, or have the bouncer do it for you.

Don't forget how important it is to smile and tip.

Don't cause problems by bringing dancers to sit at the stage with you; the girl dancing up there will think the girl sitting with you is trying to fuck up her money.

If you're at the tip rail, tip.

If you don't want to tip, then don't sit at the tip rail.

Don't insert foreign objects into any orifice or opening on a stripper's body.

The above rule includes things like your fingers, beer bottles, used chewing gum and your prick.

Don't tip the dancer on stage with quarters or any other coins.

If someone from the club asks or tells you to leave, just do it.

Never yell insults over your shoulder at the bouncers as you walk away from them across the parking lot.

Don't spend your whole dance trying to look into the stripper's eyes, it totally creeps her out.

Whenever possible, wash your hands before you get dances and always after; it's courteous to the dancer before you start, and smart for you after.

Always tip something after a dance unless it really sucked ass or she had obnoxious body odor, breath or personality.

If you accidentally cum in your pants; stop the dance, go to the restroom and get cleaned up.

If you tend to accidentally cum on yourself, wear a condom under your pants to prevent a mess.

Understand that you risk injury or death if you get your cum on a dancer.

Never yell crap at the DJ.

Don't get mad if you yelled crap at the DJ and he is now making fun of you on the microphone.

If the DJ makes fun of you on the microphone, laugh along as if you're in on the joke and it's totally cool. It's usually the best and only way to shut him up.

Don't kick, punch, shake, lean against or mess with the dj booth.

Keep smiling and don't forget to tip.

Don't argue with, or touch the manager.

Don't bother arguing with a stripper.

Don't bring irreplaceable items into the club, you'll lose them for sure and wind up divorced or something.

Don't use a camera without the express permission of the club, and that specifically includes the camera on your cell phone.

If you are asked to put your cell phone away, just do it without argument...who the fuck are you texting anyway?

Don't take your dick out unless you're in the restroom.

Don't piss in the parking lot, or against the building.

When the lights come on at the end of the night, it means leave, so go without being asked; honestly, you have better places to be anyway.

If you want a stronger drink, buy a double.

Don't think that you own the joint because it's your bachelor party, birthday party or anything else.

You aren't unique or special because you bought a bottle of liquor or champagne.

Never say, "I know the owner," especially if you do.

Make sure you know that smoking is allowed before lighting a cigarette, cigar or pipe inside the club. Ashtrays and/or matches on the table are usually a good indicator.

Remember, at the end of the day it's really just a cute girl in a skimpy bikini, and not something to stress over.

Always wear clean underwear.

If it sucks, go somewhere else.

Have fun, wipe that stupid look off your face, fucking smile...and always tip your waitress.

THREE

Playing

CHAPTER 9

The gentleman caller

NOW, A QUESTION OF ETIQUETTE...AS I PASS, DO I GIVE YOU THE ASS OR THE CROTCH?

- Abraham Lincoln, lawyer, state legislator, congressman, 16th U.S. President, vampire hunter and beard wearer; remembered for personal humility, social courtesy and love of the theater.

In the previous chapter, we talked about how a stripper is generally freaking the fuck out when she hits the floor for the first time in her shift. There are certainly exceptions to this; there are dancers who are quite unfazed by their first appearance of the night, perhaps even eagerly welcoming it.

Generally speaking, though, you can pretty much count on the fact that most girls are flipping out, even if they are adept at concealing it. This is your opportunity to stand out from the other guys in the club with basic courtesy, common sense, and a whole lot of **CONSCIOUS MANIPULATION.**

When you are in the club, and a dancer comes on the floor for the start of her shift (well, the first time you have seen her at least) you should make note of this, and keep in mind that she will be looking for a friendly face out there in the crowd to help ease her transition. This will be your chance to make a positive impression by appearing friendly and welcoming, and crucial to framing your first interactions with a stripper in whom you may be interested.

At the same time, it's essential to remain calm, gracious and undemanding about the whole thing. I've often seen men attempting to pull this move yet managing to blow it as they try to overact and grandstand their way through it. Frankly, when you overdo something like this it just comes off as irritating or even condescending.

Projecting a sense that none of this is any significant deal and honestly it's just how you are not something that you're trying to do, should be foremost in your mind. I'm not saying to act aloof and detached, as if you couldn't care less.

First of all, someone who is acting too fucking cool to talk to you isn't truly being all that welcoming, are they? Secondly, there are already a bunch of dudes in the club trying to pull game on the strippers by acting as if they are too damn cool to be there in the first place.

You and I both know that if you were way too impressive of a guy to be talking to strippers, you wouldn't be sitting in a strip club. Don't pull this move with the girls, it looks socially retarded and does nothing to help you get laid.

When a dancer first makes it out into the club proper, she will usually take a moment to survey the room to see if she recognizes anyone, and to assess the overall flow of the room. She'll be checking for obvious money customers or clear, dead-money **MARKS**. She'll want to know who is working, and where her friends or allies are, if she has any.

SEEING UNSAID

This is the chance for you to see her, and let her see you see her. If you are unsure what I mean by that, listen up. **SEEING** a woman involves looking at her in totality, as a person. You see their face, you see their body, you notice the way they are holding themselves. You notice posture, body language, the expression on their face. You see, superficially, if they are someone who takes care of themselves.

Does she lean toward or away from people? Is she listening when people are speaking to her, or just listening half ass as she texts away on her stupidly expensive cell phone with an already, inexplicably cracked screen? This is not about staring a girl down, making eye contact, or doing an up-and-down physical once-over. It's not some kind of lingering creepy **EYE-FUCKING** sort of thing.

Just take a moment to see her with your eyes, and let her see you do it. Use your **BODY LANGUAGE** to communicate your openness to interacting with her. You can do this by adjusting your body into an open, secure position facing her to whatever extent possible. Put your feet flat on the floor, with your lower legs at an angle slightly forward of your knees. Keep your chin up, chest open to view and arms relaxed at your side. Your feet should point in her direction, even if it is not possible for your torso to do so. Don't block the front of your body with your arms, keep your hands away from your face, and lean back in your chair slightly.

Don't look away in embarrassment when she catches you at this, you want her to catch you at it. When she does, just smile and go back to whatever it was you were doing before she walked out onto to the floor. If, for whatever reason, she doesn't come walking right over to you, just briefly repeat the process every few minutes.

Keep in mind that you aren't staring her down for prolonged periods, just seeing her for a few seconds (it's hard to check someone out effectively for less than 4–5 seconds; *creepy* starts happening around 9–10 seconds) before shifting your attention elsewhere, to something or someone else in easy view before returning to her once again. Eventually she'll get the picture, and come over.

In most cases, a dancer will view your friendly, yet reserved appraisal as marking your seat as an initial safe harbor as she ventures out onto the floor. This can give you the opportunity to meet strippers you don't haven't met yet without waiting for them to ambush you with some kind of hard-sell attack. Acting in a safe, inviting fashion creates the chance for you to say hello and make an impression on your own terms.

DECISIONS, DECISIONS

Another advantage to this is that normally a dancer will not hang around all that long on her first pass around the room. She is probably going to want get around to all the customers, get over to the bar, and go say something to the people that she knows. If you are appropriately greeting the girls when they first hit the floor, they will usually come talk to you for a bit, then move on to get working. That means that you don't necessarily need to get caught up in the strip club decision cycle.

THE DECISION CYCLE is the point of any club interaction in which the salesperson (a stripper) puts out a hard offer for services (dances) requiring a decision to be made by the sales prospect (you, the customer.) Getting caught too early in this process can be disastrous to the desired outcome you are actually after: forming relationships with strippers that don't involve money.

If you say yes, then you become a mark, nothing more than a source of income in other words. If you say no, then you are rejecting the dancer (spurning any woman is never a bright idea) and wasting her time. What you need is a way to postpone indefinitely having to make this decision at all. I am not suggesting that you don't get dances, or enjoy the benefits of being in a gentlemen's club with money in your pocket. After all, what would be the point of that?

What is actually required here is the ability and opportunity to hold the high ground in your interactions with the dancers, to use the services of some of them at the time of your own choosing, permanently brush others off without creating ill will, and put a select few into the category of looking but not touching. It is dancers in the last category that you will be focusing your attention on.

Getting proficient at welcoming girls as they arrive, being friendly, generous, and polite and ultimately providing some degree of safe **COMFORT** in a sea of perceived hostility and critical judgment is one essential part of that process. Doing so quickly in a manner that dictates how and when strippers can interact with you is another.

FLIPPING THE SCRIPT

Perhaps we should take a moment and get a little clearer on why you are doing this, and exactly how it's going to help prevent your relationship with a dancer from immediately devolving into a decision cycle driven money exchange. See, the thing is, every dancer out there is working a basic **SALES SCRIPT**. While there is a wide variety of possible script approaches, they are all essentially variations on a theme.

No matter how this script is presented, or how it is uniquely customized to any individual stripper's preferences and personality, it remains simply a prepared set of interactions meant to drive a sale of some kind. For the most part, this means that, despite any superficial appearances of differentiation, all the girls are going to be coming at you in the same basic way.

Functionally, a script of any kind is just a pattern, meaning that if A happens, then B. If B results in C, then go on to step D but if B does not result in C, go back to step A. It's like a flowchart, one thing leading to the next as you seek some kind of predetermined outcome.

It's all set up in an *if/then* format, as in: *If* this happens, *then* do this next. An example of what I mean would be a dancer looking at a customer and saying,

If he is alone, then go try talking to him.

If he seems to like me, then sit on his lap.

If he allows me to sit on his lap, then ask him for a dance.

It's just a type of **NESTED PATTERN**, a sales script. It's nested because it's just part of a larger part of an overall money-making pattern, which is of itself part of a pattern called stripper, which is just a part of another pattern and so forth.

We're all driven by this kind of automatic, **LIMBIC BRAIN** programming; it's not in any way unique to exotic dancers. The point, however, is that understanding that there is an unconscious pattern driving how this girl is interacting with you confers the ability to take control of the situation to your benefit.

In order to change what is happening, and to escape the **SALES FUNNEL** leading to positive engagement in the decision cycle, you must become disruptive. That is to say that your actions will purposefully **DISRUPT HER PATTERN** at any point where it normally would be both driving her behavior and informing her conscious choices.

Once a dancer has her pattern repeatedly disrupted, she will go "off script." Without this unconscious **PROGRAMMING** to back up her moves, she will be forced to improvise, act out of character and move forward without the benefit of an existing **BLUEPRINT**.

When a dancer comes out into the club, she will have certain expectations and will seek to match them up with the reality as it exists within the club at that moment. It is at this point where you will disrupt her pattern for the first time. She will then make an approach, using her script to frame her interaction with you; yet again you will disrupt her pattern.

Slightly off script at this point, she will become unsure, hesitating, her scripted behavior unable to predict what will happen next. As she joins you at your table, again you will disrupt her.

At this point, a stripper's script will no longer be particularly helpful to her, and you will have not only the initiative, but her attention, as well. Within your power will now be the ability to create your own **FRAME** for what will happen next, and she will become responsive to you, passively waiting to see what happens next.

The frame you create will itself serve as a powerful interrupt to her patterned sales script and stripper **PERSONA**, causing her to rely on a genuine, underlying identity as she is forced into a reactive posture. Since her non-stripper personality is not socialized to the club environment, she will find it difficult to relate to you as a stripper and customer, and default into woman and man modalities instead.

During any future meetings, and as your relationship develops, you will maintain this disruptive behavior, forcing your girl out of her protective stripper personality projection. You might think of this as a form of **WHITE NOISE GENERATOR** like the kind used by intelligence agents and criminals to make listening devices useless. In this same way, your mild, sustained interrupts will make your dancer's pattern inoperable and her ability to go into full on stripper mode, pushing you into the decision cycle.

In the earlier section we talked about engaging a dancer simply by seeing her from across the room, and by doing it all in an open, welcoming manner. This was your first interrupt of her pattern, albeit a relatively mild one. She came out into the showroom hoping that someone worth talking to would be there, but truly expecting the worst. Your open invitation went against expectations, playing to her vague hopes instead. This is disruptive enough to get her to focus on you as a first target, but with a level of uncertainty that you can leverage to your benefit.

HELLO, MY NAME IS

So, let's say a girl has appeared in the club, and you have used your eyes, smile and body language to convey that she would be welcome to stop by your table. She has picked up on this and finally come over to you. At this point, 95 percent of all club customers will remain in their seat, attempting to ignore the stripper until she actively makes herself known, typically by throwing herself down in his lap or putting a hand on his shoulder.

Alternatively, some customers seem to believe that acting in some way or another like a juvenile slob will attract the girl more quickly. While it is true that dancers will respond to general idiocy just as a shark responds to noise and movement in the water, it doesn't exactly endear you to them. Instead of acting like a complete jackass, you need to take control of the situation proactively.

To do this, you'll start by standing up as she arrives. Standing up like a gentleman upon the arrival of a lady will accomplish a number of things. First, it demonstrates respect for the person joining you in a social situation, and actually applies regardless of that person's gender...meaning you should do that even if we were talking about your best buddy joining you for lunch. Secondly, coming to your feet is a sign of recognition that your companion is a lady and that you are a man.

Yes, we can all have a long discussion at our *Women's Studies* tea party regarding the chauvinism involved in a man making way for the "weaker sex," and all that other crap, but I am telling you that women still appreciate **CLASSIC COURTESY**. Strippers especially can be taken off guard by this kind of thing, since their lives tend to lack those little hallmarks of conventional social courtesy.

If the dancer to whom you are speaking is incapable of appreciating this behavior, then perhaps you're talking to the *wrong girl*. Lump her in with the girls who are willing to go home with you for money, or who are known to give customers head in the VIP room…and *move your ass* on to someone else.

So, you have caught her attention, and she has responded by coming over to your table. You have stood up as she arrived, most likely to her pleased surprise. Now, make eye contact, and lightly but firmly *take her hand* for a moment (don't go for the finger-crushing good American handshake for crying out loud) and smile as she introduces herself to you.

You may be asking how you should **TAKE** a woman's hand. You will do this by reaching out to her as if to shake her hand, and as you make contact, twist your wrist gently from left to right so that your palm is facing up and hers down. Reach out with your off-hand and place it over hers so that you are essentially cupping her hand in both of yours. Introduce yourself and repeat her name back to her.

Watch, it's like this:

She walks up to your table, and you stand up and face her. She introduces herself and puts out a hand (if she doesn't do this, you may always initiate physical contact on your own by lifting your hand in the "handshake" move.) You take her outstretched hand in yours and say,

"Hello, I'm [insert your name here] it's nice to meet you."

Perhaps you think that I'm being a little ridiculous by going over this in detail, but I can assure you that guys mess this part up fairly regularly. From my own experience, I can tell you that quite a few people out there seem to think that leering suggestively, making inappropriate sexual remarks or otherwise acting like a pubescent child at a nude beach is somehow correct etiquette for introducing oneself to members of the opposite sex in a strip club.

They are wrong about that, and that is why I am forced to explain this basic crap to you.

You may now ask her to sit (she will accept, but you should still observe the formality of making the request, earning points for doing so) and move to pull out a chair for her. You will do this in the same manner in which you introduced yourself a moment ago.

As you pull out her chair, try time-tested phrases like,

"Allow me," or,

"Would you care to join me?"

This should help to keep the ball in your court and your dancer off balance. Let's take a moment and run through what we're talking about here:

Dancer approaches clearly intending to speak with you.

You stand, face her and smile.

She greets you, asks your name and puts out a hand.

You take (*not shake*) her hand and say,

"Hello, I'm [insert your name here] it's nice to meet you."

You release your grip on her hand; pull a chair out from the table and say,

"Care to join me?"

You stand behind her chair as she sits, then return to your own seat.

See, that wasn't so fucking hard, now was it?

This is how you make a first impression on a dancer...or anyone else for that matter. This will set the stage for all future interactions with the girl in question and help make you welcome any time you appear in the club. You will want to do this kind of thing with any stripper that you are interested in so that they all get a positive impression of you, one that they will reinforce amongst themselves when they talk.

Engaging in this kind of behavior will also create a **VISUAL CUE** for other dancers regarding what kind of girl you are interested in talking to. What I mean is that the girls will see how you are acting with dancer A, B and C; if you are suddenly behaving in a different, less welcoming fashion, with dancer X, Y or Z, they will start understanding who you don't want to be bothered with. This is a convenient method for **SCREENING** strippers that don't meet your criteria or pique your interest without ever having to say, "No, go away."

A great way to be clear about this, and to remain respectful and "gentlemanly," is simply to do the same thing with every dancer regardless of whether you are interested but just don't ask the girl to join you if she doesn't appear to be the kind of person that would interest you. So, a girl comes out on the floor, and you look to see if she's the right kind of dancer for you or if it's someone you already know.

She is neither, so you quit looking and focus on something else. Of course, she probably comes over anyway. When she does, you stand just as you normally would, and offer a gentle yet firm handshake. Release your grip on her hand, while saying,

"Hi, it's nice to meet you. I hope you have a good night."

And then you just sit back down without offering a chair or anything else. This should be the signal to her to move along, but sometimes dancers can be dense, obstinate or just not willing to take a soft "no" for an answer. In the event she persists, or decides to seat herself, you will need to be gently assertive. Look right at her, and use a phrase like,

"No thanks, I'd prefer to be alone right now."

THAT WAS YOUR CUE

When you do something like that it also helps to signal your intentions with the use of body language. Try tilting your torso away from the girl, sit forward somewhat on your chair, and cross one leg over another in such a way as to place your knee, shin, and foot between yourself and her. If possible, shift the orientation of your body away from the girl.

This need not be an exaggerated, clearly visible move on your part; simply allow yourself to shift slightly away from her in a subtle fashion, moving toward your open side. This is a **NONVERBAL DISPLAY** indicating that you're uncomfortable with the presence of the person with whom you are speaking and that you desire to protect the sensitive areas concentrated at the front of your torso, pelvis, and head.

If your legs are crossed, your lower body will have an **OPEN SIDE AND A CLOSED SIDE,** dictated by which leg is crossed over the other. If your left leg is crossed over your right knee, then your left side is closed, and your right side is open. If the right leg is crossed over the left knee, then the opposite is true. If you are protecting yourself from a dancer because you aren't interested in her, you should ensure that you are presenting the closed portion of your body to her. This means that your left leg, if crossed over the right knee, is displayed facing her so as to protect your open, right side.

If you don't wish to cross your legs, simply perch forward on the edge of your seat, adjust one foot (the one farthest from the stripper) so that it is oriented away, as if at any moment you might suddenly stand up and walk off in that direction.

132

Place the elbow of the arm closest to her on the table so that your arm is vertical, with your hand close to your face.

You can now use the arm to block her, and hand to shield your face. You can rest that hand across your mouth with the index finger lightly resting along your upper lip, as if you are hiding your teeth from view. Try maintaining this position even when you are speaking with her.

If you happen to be standing when an unwelcome entertainer approaches, turn away from her slightly. Make sure one foot is positioned away. If she is not getting the hint, just keep adjusting yourself farther, and farther away until eventually you are side-on to her, presenting either the left or right side of your body, (not the back or front.)

Once you have shifted into this position, called **BLADING**, adjust your feet so that they are lined up with your torso in the direction of intended travel, as if you are about to walk off at a right angle. If she is still engaging you, turn only your head toward her as you respond, keeping the rest of your body bladed to her. If this is not effective, simply say,

"Thanks, it was nice meeting you."

Then just walk off to the rest room, smoking patio, or wherever. Once you have politely shown your back to someone in this way, your meaning should become clear. If the person to whom you are speaking can't grasp what's happening on a conscious level, you can nonetheless be certain that their unconscious mind knows exactly what you just said, and will react by either giving you more space in the future, or avoiding you, if possible.

When you assert yourself in ways that I am describing, you will get the message across that you are not interested and that the dancer in question is only wasting her time by loitering around your table harassing you. The last thing you want to do when you are on the hunt for the right girl is spend all night fighting off bikini-clad *wildebeests.* Just get clear with these girls, and yourself, right from the start that you aren't interested and being an obnoxious pest will get them nowhere fast.

When you let a dancer know that you aren't interested in what she is offering, keep it polite, to the point and as friendly as you can manage. Never act in a rude manner, imply that she is not worth your time, too fat, too old, whatever. Don't pull that, *"You're just a worthless whore and beneath me,"* crap that so many guys fall back on for some reason.

Remember, you came walking into this joint all on your own; the dancer probably has the moral high ground here if anyone does, since she's just offering a service that you were actively seeking. Looking down on strippers is somewhat akin to being pissed at McDonald's for selling you a hamburger.

GETTING DANCES

I mentioned before that there is no reason not to avail oneself of all that the club has to offer, and that would include getting private dances with certain girls. The problem here is that if you get dances with a girl, you officially cross the boundary into customer territory, and everything is strictly business from this point on, no matter how pleasurable that business may be. This is like having a crush on some girl in your

134

immediate social circle but never being able to do anything about it because you are in the friend zone.

Getting dances with a stripper puts you into that same type of category, except that, in this case, you are continuously forced to pay for the privilege of getting no ass. In addition, should you ever stop paying money for the ongoing opportunity to go home perpetually frustrated and unfulfilled; she will then cut you off entirely from whatever dubious benefits may have been provided by the relationship.

There is another problem with getting, or not getting dances. If you never get any dances, the girls will all assume that you are a no-money waste of time. They will actively tell each other not to bother with you because, *"He never gets dances."* What you need to do is find a set of girls (at least two or three would be best just so that you have options, but the exact number is up to you) that you will have an enjoyable time spending money on in the dance area but never plan to do anything else with.

These dancers should be attractive, obviously fun without going so far over the line that you end up getting tossed out of the club, and easy to deal with. You do not want a girl for this that will want to call you in on slow nights or any of that kind of thing. In fact, it might be best if the girls you dance with don't have any sort of connection to you outside the club. Don't exchange numbers with this kind of girl; don't have long conversations with them, and don't sit around at your table buying drinks for them.

What you will want for your dancing partner is somebody that can walk up to your table during a dance promotion or slow time and ask for the dance, and to whom you can say yes before she even sits down. You want to be able to head to the VIP area, bang out your dances, and part ways as you exit and return to your seat. That's how painless it should be.

As I said before, once you get dances with a stripper you will cross over into customer territory with her. Everything that you do from that point forward is nothing more than a monetary transaction to her, and so it should be so for you, as well. If all you are actually doing with her is exchanging cash for services, then there is just no need to waste your time talking her up, getting to know her or any of that other crap. Plus, if you get to know her too well, it will destroy the **SUSPENSION OF DISBELIEF** that is vital to having a terrific time when she is grinding away on your lap.

Another reason why you shouldn't be hanging out talking to the girls you dance with is that it gives the other dancers the wrong impression. When they see you go down on dances with someone, they will say,

*"He is **A CUSTOMER THAT GETS DANCES** with her."*

This is an indication that you have money, do what you want with it, and are a decent person to talk to. If, on the other hand, the other dancers see you repeatedly both dancing and hanging out with the same girl, they will say,

*"He is **HER CUSTOMER.**"*

This means that *your ass* belongs to the dancer in question, and it's probably not worth their time to talk to you. They will assume that whatever money you have actually belongs to her, and that you are just another **LAME-ASS SUCKER.**

In other words, the other girls will essentially write you off until such a time as they can figure out how to wrest you away from the dancer that currently OWNS YOU, so as to get your money for themselves. You seriously need to keep this in mind when you are choosing a stripper to dance with, and always remember to keep that relationship nothing more than a fun business transaction.

PUT YOUR MONEY WHERE YOUR MOUTH IS

One other thing on that subject; if the girls you are actually interested in and spending time with see that you spend zero time with the strippers you dance with other than a quick dance or two here and there, it can put a damper on any jealousy. It also helps them to understand the **BOUNDARIES** of your relationship, and act accordingly.

Remember that you will always need to back this kind of thing up with money for the girl you are sitting with because until you emotionally hook her she will still have one eye on the clock; she is at work after all. You don't have to be rich and shower her with cash, you just need to be respectful of her time and show it with regular stage tips, and the occasional twenty dollar bill at the table.

You are also going to need to be clear with the target dancer about your intentions, at least to a point. As I mentioned before, from the moment a girl sits down with you there is an invisible timer running, inexorably counting down until the moment when she begins to make her sales pitch. This is the decision cycle that I referenced earlier. What you are going to have to do is short circuit that process before the sand runs out of the hourglass and she starts selling you.

To correct this, and to **RE-FRAME** the encounter according to your needs and intentions, is as easy as being upfront about what you want from her. Just tell the dancer that you have no intention of getting any dances but that you would love for her to join you for a while. Let her know that you understand she is working, that her time is valuable to you, and that you will respect the relationship by compensating her for the attention she is giving you. Let me show you one way to do this:

"Well, how much are the dances, $20? Honestly, I'm not looking for dances right now, but if you have a drink with me, I'll tip you the $20 up front."

In my opinion, when you are first getting to know a stripper, the best way to compensate is half up front, and half after. Offer her $20 to sit with you for the duration of a drink which you will purchase, and tip an extra $10-$20 after that drink is gone. Thank her for the time she has spent with you, make sure you are clear on her name and that she knows yours, and let her know that you are interested in talking to her again in the future.

These brief encounters should be kept somewhere in the range of ten to fifteen minutes. This time period will scale up or down depending on the speed of drink service in the club you are patronizing. It's essential to keep these meetings brief for a number of reasons, all of which are pertinent to your success here, so let's review them in some detail.

Keeping your discussion brief makes it easier to:

Maintain interest, prevent boredom

Keep the conversation focused on her prevent over intoxication (after all, it's only one drink)

Maximize the value of your compensation to her time

Prevent the appearance of monopolizing her attention

Avoid saying something stupid (since you don't have enough time in which to do so)

This is far from a comprehensive list, but I think you get the idea. Let's move on.

CHAPTER 10

It's not just a city in china

"CHEERS MATE!"

NOT AN ACCEPTABLE FORM OF TIPPING IN THE STATE OF TEXAS.

- Sign posted inside a strip club in Texas.

Tipping, that is.

You know that joke, don't you? It's funny because it's like...*Tipping*...it sounds like it would be somewhere in China, you know? But it's not about some city somewhere in China, it's actually about tipping people, and that's kind of funny. It's a play on words you see, because "tipping" and Tipping sound the same, and...ah...oh, *forget it*.

I earlier referenced the idea that you should be taking care of your entertainer for the time and effort she's investing in you. I gave the example of dropping $20–$40 on your girl over the course of a 15-20 minute conversation as you share drink together.

That's a fairly accurate overview depicting one way to take care of your girl, but it's somewhat simplistic. Since the idea of paying for a performer's time is serious enough that the idea can't simply be mentioned and left alone, as much as I wish that it could be. So let's talk more now about money, your girl, and the key protocol surrounding getting her bills paid.

One of the easiest and most recognizable forms of compensating an exotic dancer is to drop tips on her while she dances on the club stage. Tipping a dancer for her stage show is a fairly straightforward sort of thing; she takes her turn on the **STAGE ROTATION**, and you tip her in recognition of her performance.

Nonetheless, it still demands some sort of convention to perform properly, and for our purposes, not all stage tipping is created equally. There are three primary motivations for stage tipping, each with its own methodology:

Getting her attention

Focusing attention on yourself

Rewarding or reinforcing behavior

TIPPING TO GET HER ATTENTION

One of the best ways to get the attention of an exotic dancer is simply to take a seat at her stage and ante up. This puts you in **PROXIMITY** with her in a way that is acceptable, and welcome. She wants people to come to her stage and tip. Not only is it financially worthwhile for her but it demonstrates that she is exceptional, attractive and skilled at her stage show.

Trying to flag down a girl you'd like to talk to, or follow her around the club trying to get her attention can make you look like a desperate loser. Sometimes there will be no other way besides tipping her stage since she may already be sitting with another customer and not see your attention.

Going up to her stage and putting down some money will help neutralize obstacles like that. Stage tipping also gives you the indispensable opportunity to take a close look at the girl you've been eyeing from across the room.

Truthfully, it does not quite matter how much money you tip at stage side, although more is, and always will be, better. Keep in mind that strippers are surrounded all night with guys who offer cheap compliments while pinning them down with long, pointless conversations. The girls are always offered free drinks, tolerate empty declarations of love, and laugh off drunken marriage proposals. They are forced to negotiate with overweight slobs over the amount of additional service that will be provided in the course of a $20 lap dance.

In this context, it is possible to prove your **VALUE** by taking a seat at the stage with quiet confidence, while keeping your hands to yourself, and focusing on the girl center-stage with admiration and respect. If you're dropping money on stage at the right moments, materially helping pay tonight's stage fee or the cost of tomorrow's baby sitter, then you can play hero to the woman you desire, and why not?

Take a moment and just remember that, even if the girl you are tipping never develops an interest, you'll still have a fantastic time and come across to the other girls in the room as someone worthy of notice.

If you truly need to get her attention while sitting at stage side, here are a couple of tips for you: One, if the point is to get her attention, and you remain seated at the stage after she completes her set and gets off stage, it will be difficult for her to approach you effectively.

In most clubs, a dancer will make a circuit of the area after leaving the stage in order to "thank" everyone in person for their tips during her performance. This actually means she'll come by to ask the **BARGAIN MOTHERFUCKERS** who didn't tip during her set if they would now like to do the right thing, and actually thank people who already took care of her.

If you have tipped her stage, she will thank you personally at stage side as she picks up her money. As soon as this has happened, just get up and return to your table. When she does her turn around the room, she will remember you from her stage and take the opportunity to thank you again.

This will give you the opportunity to hit her up with another token tip, just to show you care. Chances are that the dancer will find her way back to you once she's walked the room. Your behavior has taught her four things:

You tipped her on stage because you like and appreciate her

You kept your hands to yourself because you respect her

You left the stage after her set because she was the only one you wanted

You tipped her again at your table because her time is valuable to you

To sum that up; you like, appreciate, and respect her, she is the only one you wanted, her time is valuable to you and you are willing to pay for it.

These are the things that are universally esteemed by all women; thus some variation of this strategy will work on any woman regardless of whether she is a stripper or not. That is to say, if the person you are employing this strategy with has female reproductive organs, estrogen, a heartbeat and an active bioelectric brain pattern that can be measured above 3Hz or so, it will work.

Be advised that your results may vary in the event said person is dead, in a coma, too old to give a fuck or, you know, *not actually a chick*.

GETTING HER ATTENTION, PART TWO

Of course, I said, *"Here are a couple of tips for you."* That was one, and here is the other: A lot of guys who sit up at the stage can get real hands-on with the girls who are just trying to shake their shit up there.

In addition, many customers will withhold tips until the dancer comes right up to them at the **TIP RAIL**. This gives the tipping customer the opportunity to put the dough into the dancer's costume, up close and personal.

When tipping a girl directly, most legal jurisdictions require that the money be placed in either a money garter (the thing dancers wear around one thigh for just this purpose) or in a non-offending clothing area.

That means that the tie-sides of the dancer's bikini bottom, normally at the hips, or in the straps of the bikini top are fine to insert a dollar into, anywhere else, legally speaking, is typically *a no-go*.

Try telling that, however, to some drunken bachelor sitting at the tip rail. Tip-related stage interactions can lead to all sorts of shenanigans when customers use their direct tipping as an opportunity to force their hands inside a dancer's costume. Even when an offending customer avoids going that far, he will still use the opportunity to run his hands along the stripper's body as she gets in close, looking to score a handful of tits and ass by "accident." In technical terms, this kind of douche-baggery is known as, **INCIDENTAL TOUCH.**

No matter what you call it though, this free molestation is just too much degrading contact for a couple of measly bucks, if you ask me. Strippers wear micro thongs and glitter to work, but that doesn't really grant you some form of blanket permission to be a dirty bastard. It most certainly won't help you attract the girl you're after unless she's a real douchebag herself. Instead of engaging in opportunistic behavior that identifies you as a complete jackass, try this method instead:

Place your tip right in front of you on the stage, and only when she has her back turned, is concentrating on another customer, or simply isn't looking in your direction.

Although this may seem counterintuitive, but I can assure you that this will be a winning move, every time. If you tip a dancer when she isn't looking, it means that you expect nothing in exchange for money. You don't need individual attention, you don't want her tits all in your face, and you don't want to put your hand down her panties as you give her a fucking dollar bill.

You are tipping for nothing more than the fact that you are sitting back enjoying her stage, and nothing more is required. Everything you need to justify a tip occurred the moment she decided to grace the stage with her presence, captivating looks, and sparkling personality. Nothing more is required; she is perfect, whole, and beautiful in every way that matters to you.

Further, you are a humble man, a simple seeker of beauty and sexual companionship, with excellent taste in women, the ability to appreciate the female form, and a gentleman's sensibilities. You need no thanks for the money you have placed before her. It is her due, and you don't begrudge that which rightly belongs to her. It was a pleasure to have shared such fleeting intimacy, no matter how illusory and putting your hands on her when something as crass as money lay between you would only ruin it. Better to share this bit of connection, and hope to meet again.

Or some such shit.

I don't actually understand why it works exactly, but it works. I'm fairly certain that you have no idea why women are **FUNCTIONALLY CRAZY PEOPLE** any more than I do, so I'd prefer you don't try giving me a ration of shit on this one. It just works. Maybe it works because all girls secretly think they're some kind of undiscovered Disney princess, or that *Mr. Right* is about to walk through the door any second now, or because they're just fucking hormone-driven psychotics. Why do you care?

A further advantage that comes along with this form of tipping is that the stripper will always be surprised when she comes by to collect the tips sitting in front of you. Most of the time, the dancer will suddenly realize that she wasn't paying enough attention to you during the **STAGE SET**.

This is guaranteed to get her off balance, make her wonder what else she might have been missing in regards to you, and force her to focus on you in the future. As your stripper suddenly realizes that you have been taking care of business while she was off in dancer *La-La Land*, she may experience an internal monologue that looks something like this:

"Could it be that Prince Charming did actually just walk in, sit at my stage, and I didn't notice because I was too busy staring at myself in the wall mirror?"

Of course, she will probably express what she is thinking as an emotional word-vomit that flashes into existence as a weird amalgam of imaginary zero-calorie cupcakes, Hello Kitty schwag, and cute, doodled hearts and stars and crap like that, filled with subtle interjections like, *OMG*, or *LOL*. No matter how she frames the moment in her mind though, the central point will remain the same,

"Wait, did I just lose money? Fuck!"

You can be sure that she will now be paying attention now while chastising herself for not doing so in the first place. If this thought should hit her just as you get up from the tip rail, turn away, and return to your seat, all the better. Your turned back retreating into the darkness represents a missed opportunity that only can be rectified if she sees you again, and curiosity regarding what other things about you that she hasn't yet noticed. When your girl walks her post-stage floor circuit, she will meet you again, this time with **ENHANCED INTEREST AND A DEGREE OF UNCERTAINTY.**

Handling your stage tipping as I have described will leave you in control and put her into a reactive mode, unsure what you are going to do next. Seizing the initiative in any way possible is an essential part of setting yourself apart from the rank and file, thus increasing your value in a dancer's assessment.

The stripper subject to this sort of attention from you will be pushed back from the attack and placed on the defense. She will be forced to invest time and attention in you in order to get what she wants money, and an easy time getting it.

Forcing an exotic dancer to stop focusing on herself and start investing in you is a master key to moving the relationship outside the club.

One last thing about tipping a dancer on stage: it's either going to be used to interrupt her pattern (she is in control and you are forced to respond by trying to get her attention) or as a means to introduce yourself. While your stage tipping could be either disruptive, or introductory, it is more often both simultaneously. Meaning, she has not been paying attention to you, therefore, you must disrupt her pattern of neglect on your own terms, and doing so affords you the opportunity to be truly seen for the first time.

Just as in any other social or business setting, it is vitally necessary that you make a favorable first impression. Always be aware of how you look, operate and behave during the times when you are tipping your girl's stage; these first meetings have the potential to set the tone for the romance to come.

TIPPING TO FOCUS ATTENTION ON YOU

Sometimes guys will walk over to the stage and throw a giant stack of dollar bills into the air so that it showers down onto the dancer, the stage, the tip rail, and other customers sitting nearby. As you probably already know, this tipping technique is known as **MAKING IT RAIN.**

First of all, if you are planning to make it rain, you should ensure that there is enough money in the stack you're planning to drop in order to generate the desired effect. There is nothing more embarrassing than watching some clueless loser try to make out like a baller as his ten or fifteen singles flutter down to the stage ineffectually.

The best way to handle this is to ask a waitress, or whoever is providing your service, to bring a fresh stack of singles in exchange for **A BILL** ($100) at a minimum. Otherwise, you are going to look like a *complete ass* up there.

It's smart to remember that one of the purposes of making it rain is to prove you have too much money to give a shit. Trying to make it rain with the wrinkled, left over change from your last drink order will only make you look like an idiot.

If you do get a fresh stack, it will be bound by a paper strap; if the money was sorted by the club it will be typically bound with rubber bands or paper clips. Whether it comes with the original paper band, rubber bands or paper clips doesn't matter all that much; just don't forget to remove that stuff.

Otherwise, you might throw your stack at the stage, only to watch in a kind of slow motion horror as it stays together in a single...*very solid*...money block that clocks the stripper you were trying to impress in the face as she hangs upside down from the pole.

If the money actually is **TREASURY-FRESH**, it will stay together even once the paper band is removed. Taking a couple of minutes to sort of fluff it up and split the bills will make sure nobody gets hurt, and you get the money shower effect you wanted.

Guys who make it rain typically go for one of two basic moves when they try to make the throw at stage side. One of these is to walk up, wait for the girl to come over, then send the money over her head, letting it rain down in a cloud over and around her.

Most guys that do it this way will usually post there for a minute, enjoying the immediate attention that has been garnered from both the dancer on stage, and the people, dancers and customers alike, who witnessed the show from their seats around the room or at the stage.

The other way to get this done is to walk up to the stage, and throw the money while simultaneously turning on one heel and heading off in the opposite direction. The point of this seems to be that it somehow proves that not only do you not care about the money but that the process of tipping is somehow beneath you and that the girl who just received the tip will need to chase you from now on since you won't be waiting around for her ass. Of course, this is fucking retarded.

While I urge you not to go engaging in this kind of base class behavior, you should know what making it rain does accomplish:

Covers up anxiety over money, success or self-image

Boosts self-esteem by suggesting you have a bigger dick

Turns public tipping into an aggressive action that demonstrates strength

Permits the enjoyment of public degradation of others

Screens dancers for their willingness to accept degradation and abuse

Asserts sexual dominance over other males

I am pretty sure that this tipping trick is useful to some people. I am equally sure that there is a kind of dancer who responds in a tremendously positive way to this type of customer interaction. It would not at all be hard for you to find dancers who will tell you how much they love it when a customer makes it rain for them.

Despite how harshly I am treating this behavior, I will concede that in some places, at some times, with some people, making it rain can be a positive thing, and perhaps, for the right customer, it can be the key that will unlock the right stripper's heart.

This book and my advice, information and strategies, are not designed for that place, that time, those people, that customer, or that stripper, however. **SEXUAL DOMINANCE** behavior, often learned in correctional facilities, and propagated by pop cultural stereotyping, will not result in positive, successful relationships with adult entertainers.

I have seen dancers develop relationships with guys who routinely engage in making it rain, and other related behaviors, but I have never seen those relationships be anything other than something trivial based solely on money.

Superficial attraction based on dominance behavior and the exploitation of the inner crisis within most exotic entertainers is unhealthy and generally *un-fucking-cool*. Further, it is clearly not what we are going for with all this. Tipping to focus attention on you, and to establish dominance is not a winning strategy. At best, it is an indication of an immature, **INSECURE MALE PSYCHE** that can offer little of real value to a woman, and does little to advance your cause.

Plus, all women want a man who will focus on them, and their needs. How can you do that for someone else when your primary goal is to get people to pay attention to you?

MAKING IT RAIN: THE REVERSE

There is one reversal to my advice here that is worth going over. There may be times when you unconditionally want to show your financial commitment to the stripper you are pursuing. Making it rain could be a powerful way to do that in an unexpected, spontaneous fashion but how to get around the selfish intent normally associated with tipping like that?

How do you somehow remove yourself from any negativity related to your dancer needing to crawl around picking up a bunch of dollar bills scattered all over the stage?

Easy, *don't do it yourself*. Call a waitress over, explain that you would like her to make it rain on your behalf, give her money, and tip her in consideration of her assistance. Tip well to ensure that things get handled correctly.

Ask the server to bring the dancer a bucket for the money when the stage set ends, and to help her get the money off the stage and safely into the bucket so it doesn't end up being a stressful event, or hold up the introduction of the next dancer on stage.

If handled in this way, all of the negativity associated with making it rain just simply disappears. In its place, you have the stage dancer reacting with pleasant surprise, more excitement in the room as the money rains down, the sight of one attractive woman throwing fistfuls of money at another, followed by a rapid clean-up and transition to the next stage set.

Your stripper girl doesn't need to feel self-conscious about picking the money up, since there is a friendly staff member up there lending a helping hand. Even the waitress will feel valued, since she made quick money doing something fun and exciting.

The best part of doing it this way is that you can accomplish all this without ever getting up, drawing attention to yourself, or acting like a *self-centered asshole*. Your dancer will still undoubtedly know who gave her money, and your modesty will score you additional points.

This is something that I would not do every day, of course, but **SOMETIMES A MOMENT OF EXCESS CAN PAVE THE WAY FOR LASTING SUCCESS.** I would reserve this for birthdays, specific instances where you know your girl needs to feel special, or because you hit the lottery and care to share.

In the beginning of this chapter, I mentioned three reasons for tipping out a dancer. So far we have discussed two of them:

getting her attention and getting attention focused on you. The final reason for tipping out is to reward or reinforce positive behavior on the part of the stripper-girl you are dealing with.

This kind of tipping will generally occur on a private or semiprivate basis, and how much, for what, when and in what way you pay her will form an association between her prosperity and success, and what kind of guy you are, for better or for worse, fair or not. This topic deserves its own separate treatment and attention, so we'll handle it in the next chapter.

CHAPTER 11

Rewards for good behavior

I AIM TO MISBEHAVE.

- Malcolm Reynolds: from the film, "Serenity."

In the last chapter, we spent time discussing tipping opportunities, situations and methods. We covered the concepts of tipping out a dancer in order to attract her attention, something you would do while she has the stage. We also went over the idea of tipping to focus attention on you, attracting strippers, staff and other customers in order to generate an aura of false dominance.

The final stripper-tipping fundamental is the intention to reward and reinforce positive behavior on the part of dancers with whom you are interacting. This method of compensation is the strategic tool that allows an entertainer to become **HABITUATED, SECURE, AND ALIGNED** with you. It is something you must do correctly in order to be successful in your endeavor to cross over from club fantasy to personal reality.

The funny thing is that getting this part straight is not, strictly speaking, all that difficult. I'm sure you've heard the phrase, *"It's not rocket science,"* haven't you? Well, I'm here to tell you that it's not...*you know*...rocket science, dammit. Yet, somehow dumb-ass dudes sitting in strip joints manage to get this wrong time and time again.

Taking care of the financial needs of exotic dancers is such a fundamental, base-level task that fucking it up screws over every other part of your **CUSTOMER GAME**. If you are the best looking, most snappily dressed guy in the club, yet dancers avoid you like the plague, I can almost guarantee you have some totally wrong and downright dipshit idea about providing for your girl that is blowing everything. Tipping out dancers is straightforward, easy, and satisfying in its way. Let's handle that now.

TIPPING TO REWARD OR REINFORCE BEHAVIOR

So far, we have focused on tipping girls mainly during their stage sets, although making it rain often gets used when a dancer is off stage, as well.

Now we need to shift our attention to the ongoing reward and reinforcement of positive behaviors exhibited by your dancer, specifically those behaviors that will occur offstage. This is the absolute short list of behaviors that you continuously need to reward or reinforce as they occur:

Spending time at your table

Checking in after a stage performance

Giving you something for free

Choosing you over another customer

Spending time in a private or vip area

In order to reward your dancer for engaging in a desirable behavior, you have to get in the habit of tipping out to her so that she will come to associate the action with the tip. By doing so, what she may initially perceive as a straightforward **PAYMENT FOR SERVICE** will rapidly become an obvious reward.

An entertainer who is paying attention will quickly come to understand what you like or don't like, and may attempt to the game your system by repeating "good" behavior in order to stimulate additional tipping on your part. She may think she has you figured out and knows the formula to wring every last dollar from you.

It's perfectly reasonable for her to think that; doing so will create lasting associations between what you want, and what she wants. It does not matter if she has you, "figured out," the **UNCONSCIOUS ASSOCIATIONS** connecting the behavior that you desire and the money that she wants will be extremely real.

Essentially, by attempting to beat you at your own game, a dancer can unwittingly end up training herself to respond positively to your presence, your needs, and most importantly, to your desires. The effect will still remain the same, even if she doesn't figure out your game straightaway.

Just be aware that it may take longer to get results this way, although it will certainly cost you less. It will take longer to achieve results in this fashion, but that is only because her misunderstanding of your tipping behavior does not provide as many opportunities for the required associations to form. From that standpoint, it can be better if she does figure out what you're doing, even if it does hit you in the wallet somewhat harder.

SPENDING TIME AT YOUR TABLE

So, if she sits with you over the course of a drink, make sure she walks away with $20-$40 for her time. It's a fair exchange, she won't regret the time so long as you didn't bore her to death, and she will come back again, especially if you have requested that she do so. If she hangs around longer than the time it takes to share a drink, simply continue tipping as you have been using the rule of **$20 FOR TWENTY** the entire time she remains with you.

In other words, make sure you lay down another $20 for every twenty minutes she spends with you. Remember, the goal here is not to bankrupt yourself trying to impress her with your bankroll, the actual point is to compensate her for the time she is investing in you. Feel free to adjust the amount as you see fit, as your finances allow, and as your girl deserves.

Adjust up, that is; $20 should be considered your default, base-level. If you can't swing the $20, you'll have a hard time keeping her attention, and you probably can't afford to be playing this game anyway.

Be wary of over tipping for her time, as this may have the unintended result of instilling unrealistic expectations regarding money. Ideas about money, compensation, and the quantifiable worth of her time for fairly pedestrian activities such as sharing a drink or brief conversation can carry over into your outside relationship later on, so be careful what your actions related to money and spending teach her.

CHECKING IN AFTER A STAGE PERFORMANCE

You'll always want your dancer checking back with you after she gets off stage. There are multiple reasons to get her to do this, and they are all to your benefit.

She stops wandering off in the middle of your time together

She checks with you before dancing with someone else

She checks with you before going social with another guy

She starts keeping you informed about what she's doing

She views your seating area as a logical start and end point

You don't need to sit there wondering if she is coming back

You can make future plans or just leave without waiting

All of this happens mainly on an unconscious level, and there is little or no reason to discuss these things directly. When she swings back to your table on her post-stage circuit around the showroom, lay your minimum tip out on her, while saying something both genuine and positive regarding her performance.

If you have been hitting her with $20 for 20 for the past hour while you were sitting together, make sure her stage tip is at least $20. If you have time (and the desire) to hang out for a while more, let her know that you want her back as soon as she is done walking the room.

If you have a **TIME CONSTRAINT**, let her know about it but emphasize that you want her back before you leave. If you don't have a time constraint, make a plausible one up, and again, let her know you want her back before you leave. Please keep in mind that you must respect the validity of a fake obligation just as if it were real, otherwise the dancer will start thinking she doesn't need to respect your time, real life or outside interests.

After all, you said you had to leave at 10pm, but now it's one o'clock in the morning, and you're still here. If you don't care about the things you have to do, or that you say are necessary, why should she?

If waiting for stripper-girl to return from her *thank-you-tip-me* walk is something that you can't or won't do, just let her know that you'll see her the next time around and make sure you find out when the next time will be.

It's actually smart for you to refuse to wait occasionally, simply choosing instead to end your meeting on a high note. Of course, there is a difference between refusing to wait, and employing an excuse for your departure. Simply refusing to wait is a reminder that little stripper girl is not actually the center of the universe, even if she doesn't know it yet.

Remembering this from time to time benefits you as well, serving to take the edge off things when you get too caught up in the moment. Refusing to wait for her can also help to habituate your dancer to the idea that she needs to work to keep your attention at all times; otherwise you may suddenly just decide that it's time to go.

On the other hand, utilizing a **FICTIONAL OBLIGATION** (an excuse to leave) is a way to push back from the table without appearing rude or abrupt while simultaneously indicating that you do have a life outside of the club and that your time spent there is at least equal in importance to that spent inside the club.

Not only does the idea that you may have pressing business elsewhere act to increase your perceived social value, but it is also somewhat **REASSURING** to any female. After all, if you have nothing to do, and nowhere to go except hanging out in strip clubs, how useful of a guy could you actually be?

GIVING YOU SOMETHING FOR FREE

Sometimes your dancer will come straight with you, giving you something for free. This could be any number of things; an extra dance at no charge, for example. Other things that could wind up free include drinks, free passes, a free entry sign-in at the door, a gift on your birthday or at Christmas, a souvenir from her recent trip to Cabo San Lucas, or just what the fuck ever.

The most notable aspect of this kind of behavior is that it demonstrates an ability on her part to think outside the, "I dance, you pay," box, a capacity to think of you when it is not strictly necessary, and a desire to please you.

This is the kind of thing that should be rewarded without delay, and encouraged whenever possible. Yet, making too large a deal of it tends to diminish the importance of the act, and, in the case of some dancers, may serve only to discourage such behavior in the future.

While this may sound a bit odd, just take a moment to think back to when you were a kid. I'm sure that at some point, as you were headed to make your bed (or whatever) your mom called out to you with a reminder that your bed needed to be made.

Then, inexplicably, instead of pleasing your mom by doing something you were already going to do, you simply turned the opposite direction and headed outside instead. Do you remember that, or something like it? Why did you do that, do you even know?

While I'm not exactly sure why we all pull that kind of crap, I think it has something to do with people, not wanting to be told to go do something when they were already doing it. After all, telling someone to do something that they already would have done all on their own robs that person of the pleasure of accomplishing the thing that they were just about to do. *Try saying that five times fast.*

I think that we all derive value and fulfillment from handling our own shit, acting like grown-ups, and making our own way. When somebody tells you to go do what you were already going to go do on your own...well, it just ain't the same.

Looked at from that perspective, telling teenagers to go handle their shit is probably the worst thing a parent could do; adolescents are **BIOCHEMICALLY HARDWIRED** to tell you to go fuck yourself when you ask them to load the dishwasher.

In case you haven't noticed yet, most strippers are perpetual teenagers, mostly remaining that way until their dancing days are long behind them. For the implications of that, see *dishwasher* and *go fuck yourself*, above.

With that in mind, you are going to need to handle this sort of reward with a touch more circumspection than usual in order to avoid any unnecessary complications.

Still, like everything else I keep telling you, it's not quite as hard as it sounds. Follow me on this one; your dancer brings you a gift, like a cat leaving a half-dead parakeet on your doorstep:

DO

Accept the gift

React with mild surprise (fake it)

Remain speechless for a moment (this gives you a moment to think)

Say something genuine, positive, and brief about the item

DO NOT

Exclaim loudly

Jump up, and down in excitement

Go around showing it to other people in the club

Spam all your facebook friends with multiple images of the item

THEN

Allow her to tell you all about how and why she got this for you

Focus on her, and smile at the appropriate moments in the story

Make brief physical contact (taking her hand, for example.)

Say, "thank you."

At this point, enough time has probably elapsed that you would normally lay down a tip, and this case is no different. Lay down your tip just like usual, but double the amount. Make no reference to it, don't look at it, mention it out loud or invite her to notice that there is more on the table than she is used to.

Don't worry about whether or not she directly noticed that your compensation increased in association with the **GIFTING BEHAVIOR**; dancers always count their money. Your girl will see that she has picked up more than normal from you tonight but will have a hard time making a directly verifiable connection, leaving her only with generalized associations to take away from her meeting with you.

In other words, she gave you something, and you were appreciative without being a fag about it. She felt happy about giving, and you didn't ruin it by immediately tossing a bunch of cash in her face. Further, she did something neat, everyone felt valued, and in the end she walked away with more money than normal.

That's a *win-win*, and she'll likely to do it again if the opportunity arises. As your relationship progresses, she may even actively seek opportunities to engage in gifting behavior like this.

Always reward, and act with class so as to preserve the moment on her behalf. Remember, giving is more about the giver than anything else, in every social situation, whether inside the club or not. Act right, reward, make investing in you fun for her...and pretty soon you'll be opening Christmas presents together in your own living room.

CHOOSING YOU OVER ANOTHER GUY

This is actually an easy one. Occasionally you will find that you are competing for the time and attention of your girl with some other dude. Perhaps he will be an established customer of hers that she doesn't wish to offend; other times he may simply be a strong prospect, or someone who was dancing and tipping heavy with her before you walked in.

The first correct thing for you to do in this situation is relax, and simply let go of the outcome. If she's busy, make sure you make contact and verify that she knows you're there. Shoot her a text, or use the stage tipping strategy from Chapter 9. Now give her a couple minutes to respond without stressing it. Do not, *under any circumstance*, start **TEXT-SPAMMING** her.

If she doesn't get to you within ten minutes or so, blow her ass off. Don't hesitate, and be prepared to take the next step. Doing so will require you to either, a) *immediately leave*, or b) *go down on dances* with another girl as soon as you possibly can. For clarity, the phrase *as soon as you possibly can* actually means *right fucking now* in English.

Once you wrap that up, move your business to some other dancer if your girl isn't waiting for you with a pissed off look on her face. If she is waiting for you, as she should be, then simply explain that you needed to keep yourself occupied while she was busy. Let her chew on that for a bit and see how it tastes.

If she's not ready for you after you wrap it up with the second girl, then **BLOW HER OFF** and go home. You have better things to do with your life than wait around for some dime store stripper to get off some other dude's jock.

She needs to know that; frankly so do you. Don't ever throw a bitch fit when you walk out. Just leave in a way that suggests that it's the most natural thing in the world, and you certainly couldn't care less.

Of course, that's actually just what to do when your dancer fucks up. The real point, however, is what to do when she gets it right. If you were to encounter a competitor that is attempting to use your girl's time, and she responds by clearly making a choice to spend her time with you instead, then you need to **REWARD TO REINFORCE** the idea that the choice she made was the right one.

As in the other examples I have given, just wait until the moment when you would normally tip, and then go heavy with it without being too overt; she'll get the message without you needing to post a sign about it.

Further, you want this to be a soft association that allows her to be pleasantly surprised by her take on the night she decided to choose you…as opposed to the idea that you paid her to blow someone else off. Simply adding to the routine tip closest to when she picked you over someone else, without fanfare or any discussion will accomplish this.

Don't try to add in the extra scratch at the end, as you part ways for the night. Though she'll certainly appreciate the extra money, you may fail to make the connection needed to reward her positive behavior, and maybe next time she'll choose differently, even though you paid her more.

Also, keep in mind that there may be multiple occasions in the course of any time spent with her that she may be faced with this choice. If she is choosing correctly, then reward. As in all other things, there is no cause for this to break the bank on your end. If she BURNS a loyal customer for you, then at least double up your normal tip.

Ignoring some guy who wanted to go get a **TWO-FOR-ONE** dance is a little less critical, so just toss in a few extra bucks. It's necessary to watch for this kind of behavior so that your reward comes quickly after the **OBSERVED BEHAVIOR** itself. After all, any woman that would blow off other guys for your dumb ass is worth money as far as I'm concerned.

Finally, know that choosing you over another guy is a **WEIGHTED BEHAVIOR**. What I mean is that while it's a positive behavior, but it doesn't always necessarily apply equally to everyone. The rule is pretty straightforward; the more you are worth, the less this behavior means. Conversely, the less you are worth, the more this behavior means.

In other words, if you have a load of cash and she knows it, blowing off other men may not mean all that much, since she's probably going to invest her time with you anyway. But if you're close to broke and she's only got eyes for you, you better damn tip because this girl likes you better than money...And if some girl likes you better than money, drop everything, buy a ring and fucking *propose to her before someone else does, you idiot.*

SPENDING TIME WITH YOU IN THE VIP

We're going to go over the mechanics of VIP areas in the next chapter, so I'll be brief here. Taking a girl into a VIP dance area creates an opportunity to get some private time with your stripper and does so in a way that allows her to stop worrying about money, relax and **BUILD COMFORT** with you.

It allows you the chance for greater physical contact within limits, which is, in and of itself, a particularly fundamental part of creating **CONNECTION** between two people. The VIP experience allows two people to talk without shouting and tends to block interference from club staff, her competitors, and other guests (otherwise known as your *competitors.*)

In the next chapter, we will discuss how all this works, and specifically how you will use the VIP dance experience itself as a way of tipping. For the moment though what I want to get across to you is that despite whatever you might pay for the VIP booth area, associated beverage purchases and fees to the dancer who is joining you there, it's not tip inclusive.

Don't *assume* that you covered her because you paid the fee. In actuality, a big chunk of the money you're going to drop in the VIP area will ultimately end up in the hands of the club; therefore, you're going to need to make up some of the difference for her so she doesn't come out short.

There is no hard and fast rule regarding the specific amount you need to send her way but there is a scale you can use to judge whether to tip up, down or just check the box with some minimal consideration. And, once again, it's a little bit counterintuitive. The more sexual, transaction oriented the VIP experience is, the less you should tip.

On the other hand, the more relaxed, connected, conversational the experience is, the more you should tip. Remember, the point of this is not to get a hard grind in a dance booth. The point is to meet, and form a connection with a girl that ultimately becomes your new, hot stripper girlfriend. If all she wants to do is take your money and **GRIND IT OUT** until the music stops, then she is the wrong girl.

You're looking for a girl who can sit beside you or on your lap, someone that you can put your arm around casually. You want to be able to relax with her, and just hang out without any of the time you spend together seeming weird or awkward.

You want to be able to use the relative quiet of the VIP area to carry on a real conversation, and be able to enjoy doing so. You want to feel her leaning against you in a natural way, and you want to see her normal defenses relax if not drop entirely.

When you make some physical contact, you want to feel arousal, while still being able to laugh at some dumb shit she just said. If this is what you get, if this is the side of her that she shows you in private, then fucking tip for it. If you get anything less, then tip less.

If she just climbs on top of you and grinds it out without looking at you, then don't sweat the tip. Let the fees you paid cover it, and don't bother talking to her again *because she's wasting your time.*

CHAPTER 12

Affordable pleasures

THIS NEXT GAME WAS INVENTED BY DOUBLE-JOINTED HUNGARIAN ACROBATS FROM THE MUNICH CIRCUS.

- Phineas Taylor Barnum, showman, businessman, scam artist, entertainer, state legislator, mayor of Bridgeport, Connecticut, and widely credited with inventing mermaids.

You need to be on the ball where money and half-naked women are concerned, but there is certainly no need for the whole thing to break your ass financially. You should never allow a situation that has negative financial consequences for your life outside the club. Never make paying your dues in the club something that is a hardship, or could hurt you.

Exercise sound judgment when it comes to balancing the financial reality of life's obligations with your desire to indulge in the pleasure that only soft, giggly girls in undersized bikinis can provide. Listen to me closely now,

If you can afford to be in the club, then you can afford to pay the girls.

Take a moment and truly let that one sink in. If you are sitting in a club, stressing over your money, budgeting shit out, complaining about how the strippers and the club itself are fucking you over, raping you blind...*then you shouldn't even be there*. Seriously go home with that shit. If you want to complain over things, it should be the quality of the girls, level of service, how safe the club is, the fact that you just stepped in gum again, or that the toilets don't work right.

Maybe it seems that strip joints are places you go to see a show involving women stripping out of their clothes, and acting as if they like you. It seems that way because that's what it looks like. The truth, however, is that **LIVE ADULT PAY-PER-VIEW EXPERIENCE** is a far more accurate way to describe the actual business model that underlay every strip club you've ever heard of.

You pay outrageous cover charges, inflated drink prices, surcharges on the use of ATMs, credit cards, and club money sold in the form of poker-style chips or funny money club script. You are expected to tip everyone, and pay for the time of the women that entertain you. Voluntarily walking into a place like this with money in your pocket, and time to spare, makes a statement. And that statement goes something like this,

"Why is there so much money in my pockets? If only there were a place with loose women, overpriced booze, and loud music where I could spend it! Holy crap! A strip club! Problem solved!"

When someone enters the darkened interior of the local strip club, is this exactly what's going through their mind? Honestly I have no idea what you weird people are thinking, but I'd lay bets that I'm on the money there or close to it. In my experience, a person walking into a club is generally performing a feat of mental gymnastics that involve the use of *false or unrealistic variables* in the resolution of an internalized algorithm dictating the perceived **MINIMIZATION OF COST AND THE MAXIMIZATION OF OUTCOME.**

Wait, what?

This is one of those things that sound far more complicated than it is. The concept behind cost minimization and outcome maximization is that we all desire to generate the greatest potential output, or the most ideal outcome for the absolute lowest cost that is theoretically possible.

This is a totally logical, useful **COGNITIVE PROCESS** that the average human uses multiple times per day without being aware of it, or knowing what to call it. Let me give you some examples to illustrate what I mean,

> *1. If, starting at age 30, I invest $500 per month in a savings plan that earns 7.5% interest, I will retire at age 65 as a millionaire.*
>
> *2. If, starting today, I purchase a $1 lottery ticket every time I stop at the store, I will become a millionaire soon.*

Statement #1 represents a cost/outcome statement that utilizes verifiable input variables, while #2 employs faulty or unreliable variables. The second statement uses unrealistic variables because it seems easier, despite the supremely real fact that doing so makes it damn near impossible to achieve your stated outcome (to become a millionaire.) The conscious mind just totally loves things that seem easy and is quickly seduced by absolute belief in **REASONABLE FALSEHOODS.** After all, you could win the lottery, couldn't you?

The truth of the above cost/outcome statements is that #1 is actually the easier of the two. It says that by taking this quantifiable action (investing $500 per month), starting here (at age 30), and ending there (when I am 65), and with predictable variables (an insured savings instrument with 7.5% return), then this outcome (retiring as a millionaire) is guaranteed.

But spending 30 years scraping $500 together to stick in my savings every month for the promise of some future payoff doesn't quite seem all *that* easy, does it? Far better gambling some spare change on the **MEGA MILLIONS** every time I stop by the store for coffee, cigarettes and Twinkies. This, of course, explains why we all spend considerable time and energy conducting extensive, diligent analysis that informs our vital life decisions...*then chuck it all* out the window as we make up our minds using the logic from statement #2.

It's something close to that second statement that runs through the head of guys going to joints on any given night. Somehow, in some way, they *just know* that they are going to end up drowning in free pussy down at the club. When that doesn't happen, and they're called out to pay for their shit, most dudes tend to get all bent out of shape, demanding to see a manager, wanting to call the cops, *needing a hug from their mommies.*

What I am trying to get across to you with all this is that you need to adjust your expectations to align with actual reality, set hard boundaries on the level of time you can invest, work within the financial limitations imposed by real exterior obligations, and train yourself to maintain control, to be present and self-aware at all times.

If all you actually want is to head out with the boys for a night of drunken party hijinks, then by all means go right ahead and ignore everything I've been telling you because it doesn't relate to your goals. But if you want to solo mission your favorite gentleman's club with the intent of bagging a stripper girlfriend, then you need to be **ALIGNED AND CONGRUENT** with a different way of presenting yourself to others, and interacting with the girls in a responsible, adult fashion.

I do not at all want to confer the false idea that you need to be Daddy Warbucks, Donald Trump or Scrooge Mc-*Fucking*-Duck in order to get down and have an enjoyable time at your local strip joint. You can totally enjoy the show, have a few drinks, spend time with the girls, and still make it home with money in the bank, and time to sleep before work tomorrow. *Or* you can drink until you black out, get your ass kicked by security, go on a permanent stripper shit list, and wake up the next day with an empty bank account and no job because you slept in past noon again.

Just get clear before you head down to the club that you will pay to play, and on any occasion where you cannot or will not be able to pay, you will just stay home and jerk off to crappy free porn clips on the Internet instead. This is just how the real world works, and you'd better get used to it now, or you're likely to spend more than a few nights crying yourself sleep over the blatant unfairness of it all. As the comedian Denis Leary once said, "Life sucks, buy a helmet."

Every stripper you've ever met has been on the job working at the time that you met them. They're not dating, hanging out at a singles mixer, or hoping to get lucky tonight. They're not trying to get laid in the VIP with some dude they've known for less than an hour, and stripping is neither charity nor community service.

The fine ladies over at the **BYOB GIRLIE JOINT** across the county line out on *old Route 6* aren't a bunch of desperate sluts just waiting around for a chance to throw their pussies at you for free, although it may be kind of entertaining to think so. Girls who work *need to get paid.* Maybe that sounds a little cutthroat but just remember that a dancer works to earn what may be the sole source of income, not just for herself, but for her kids, as well.

There are only so many hours in any given shift, and you can only do so many dances in any given hour. There is an upward limit on the productive capacity of a stripper during any given working period, and most dancers will have *little patience* for a **NO-MONEY CUSTOMER** when rent on the apartment comes up in two days, and the car note just went thirty days past due.

A generally well-known way to compensate a dancer for her time is one in which the customer takes on the role of a **SUGAR DADDY**. In this method, the customer assumes a large portion of the responsibility for the financial well-being of a particular pet dancer.

The Sugar Daddy provides a cell phone, usually as an extension of his own contract. This gives the girl a free phone with no monthly cost or contract hassle, but it also gives her customer access to her, ability to track her phone, and pull her phone records. The stripper gets her rent paid, or even has an apartment provided on the customer dime.

Sometimes "Daddy," will pay for a car, or loan his pet stripper an extra car (usually his wife's, oddly) on a semi-permanent basis. A guy using the Sugar Daddy strategy will go out on

MONEY DATES during which there will be *large* sums spent on expensive meals, and entertainment; not to mention the requisite shopping for clothes, jewelry, and cosmetics.

In exchange, the Sugar Daddy customer will have extraordinarily high expectations for access to the dancer not only in the club environment, but off venue, as well. This access must be granted unless the stripper wants the rent money to come up short, or watch as a couple of guys in a tow truck come pick up the loaner car she had started thinking of as hers. Once a dancer becomes this dependent on a customer, the situation *will* escalate until it includes sex.

Many girls will refuse sex *initially*, attempting to wrest one more shopping trip out of the situation, or get one last bill paid. At some point, it will become a put up or shut up situation that forces things across the line into what is essentially **PROSTITUTION**. If a dancer refuses to cross that line, the arrangement will suddenly terminate, typically in the most awkward fashion imaginable.

When the cops show up looking for a stolen vehicle, reported missing by a customer who's been playing *Sugar Daddy* with some hapless dancer, you can almost guarantee that somebody didn't get the return on their investment that they felt was owed them. It's at times like these that the best you can do is let the dancer cry it out, while offering gentle reminders that this may be for the best; after all, that car only ran on **BLOWJOBS** anyway.

The Sugar Daddy approach is often employed by a high rent version of the *Sucker* customer (we talked about them earlier, remember?) We'll call him the **BIG MONEY** customer, and he's just like any other Sucker, but with more resources. He tends to enjoy more *relative power* in his dancer dealing than the typical Sucker, since the girls who depend on him will have a lot more to lose.

The Big Money has a decent **BANKROLL**, resources to support his pet dancer, high expectations, and demands that *must* be met. Big Money successfully uses the Sugar Daddy methodology, but will be unable to match an actual, full-time Sugar Daddy in scale and investment.

Whether you are a Sugar Daddy or just Big Money, it all comes down to **BUYING PUSSY**. Seems like it would be ever so much easier just to hire an escort for the evening, but how the fuck do I know? I suppose that guys who are pursuing this path aren't *actually* buying sex so much as they are buying a sexually desirable, **OFF-THE-SHELF GIRLFRIEND**. If this is your thing, by all means knock yourself out. But if you have the money to buy the girl outright, you won't need a book like this to help you along the way.

As I have already said numerous times, what goes on in the club is a fantasy and *should be kept there*. Your pursuit of the hot dancer that will make your friends envy you generally *won't fare well* in the light of day, or when you take her shoe shopping at the local mall. Determine instead to win the heart of your dancer inside the club, and maintain the separation between fantasy and reality even when she has become yours in the off hours.

Mostly, you can't follow the Sugar Daddy or Big Money path and expect your pet to think of you as a potential soul mate *anyway*. Perhaps that appears to indicate a lack of gratitude on the part of strippers who benefit from such an arrangement, but it actually demonstrates that dancers are quite capable of **PERCEPTIVE CLARITY** where other people are sometimes blind.

At the heart of things, strippers know Sugar Daddy types for what they are; a mobile financial resource that can be activated whenever needed in exchange for a *limited* time investment and *tolerable* physical contact. An ability to be realistic and a propensity for tolerating moderate levels of unpleasantness in the course of achieving lifestyle goals should not be mistaken for actual love, affection or as a statement of preference, however.

If you go this route, you forfeit the goal of overcoming the highly tuned defenses of an exotic entertainer, winning her heart outright as she hunts for the next money mark within the relative security of the club that she calls home.

Know this; every woman in the world can be bought.

That's not meant as sexist commentary, it's simply a statement of clear reproductive imperatives that guarantees the survival of the species. Women will always be susceptible to high levels of perceived security in potential male partners; it's the best way to ensure that your offspring can reach adulthood without being eaten by **A SABER TOOTH TIGER**.

Guys who can walk into the club and make all of your money problems disappear with a wave of a black *American Express* card are satisfying that requirement even if they happen to be less desirable than other men in a physical sense.

Is hooking up simply a matter of money and resources? Maybe so, but only if you assume "money" refers to some arbitrary quantity, and "resources" must be those associated with financial wealth, property ownership or intellectual rights.

If you have money to pay the cover, if you have money to buy her a drink, if you have money to tip her on stage, if you have money to tip at your table, if you have money to pay for a dance, then **YOU HAVE MONEY.** And while you may suffer from a lack of certain physical resources, *it won't matter* if you focus on being, thinking and acting with resourcefulness.

The quality of **RESOURCEFULNESS** is not a possession to be bought and sold, and it is not conferred by right of birth or decree. Being resourceful cannot be taken away, or lost by accident; it's not the byproduct of luck, or chance, and it does not become old, irrelevant, or go out of style. If you cultivate the quality of resourcefulness, then *you have resources*.

STOP HERE,

Lean in close,

And understand this:

You have enough money to compete

You are as resourceful as you want to be.

Women don't want to be bought

They want to be won, and you can win this game.

SO GO FUCKING WIN.

FOUR

Winning

CHAPTER 13

There's no sex in the champagne room

WHAT EXTRAS DO YOU DO IN THE CHAMPAGNE ROOM?

NONE.

WHAT DO YOU MEAN BY NONE?

- Overheard conversation.

There's no sex in the Champagne Room...or so Chris Rock would have us believe.

Is he correct? Well, the experience is going to be different for everyone and, as they say, your mileage may vary (or **YMMV** in online postings and text messages) but if I were a betting man I would probably take odds that Chris Rock knows a thing or two about trying to get laid in the Champagne Room.

I think that I already said this, but *don't do dances*, at least not with a dancer you need to get all serious with. As we already talked about, doing dances tends to leave you squarely in the **CUSTOMER-ONLY** category. In other words, the girl gets accustomed to you being someone she trades with; *her* sexuality for *your* money, something which is not *exactly* the same thing as trading sex for money.

JUST A JOHN

Becoming someone that purchases intimate contact from her will not make you a potential boyfriend, it will just make you into someone who buys shit from her; **A CUSTOMER**. Worse still, you may be seen as a guy who wants sex without first proving his worth, demands sex without regard to a woman's feelings and pays for sex if necessary. If you feel that way, what must you think about her? Is this girl you claim to love some kind of a **HOOKER**, is that what you think?

Do you respect, love or remain loyal to a hooker? Do you provide for the safety, well-being, and security of a hooker beyond what you leave on the bedside table when you're through? The girl you are dancing with may think that if you are willing to pay for this level of intimacy with her, you'll be more than happy to do it with other girls, as well.

Regularly dancing with a stripper you are trying to hook up with may oddly result in being deemed untrustworthy. Of course, that doesn't suggest that you could *never* enjoy the thrill of a private lap dance with an entertainer you're trying to pull, just don't do it regularly.

Sometimes you might get a dance with a girl only to realize she's the one you're interested in. People have a tendency to meet like that in strip clubs because the environment is structured to encourage introductions in the dim lighting of a private dance area, so neither of you should be overly bothered by it. If this is the case, then just switch tracks with her after the opening dance encounter concludes.

From this point on, you will not be her dance partner, and you will not buy her desire. What you will do is compensate her for the time she spends entertaining you, and, for most dancers that will be perfectly acceptable. Given a choice between being handed cash for sharing your company over the course of a drink, or going to the back room so that she can rub all her soft bits across your rough jeans for the same money, the majority of entertainers will select the drink-and-light-conversation option.

MAKE THE MOVE

Still, sharing a certain amount of privacy, in a quieter, more intimate setting, is not only entertaining in its own right, but beneficial to your game. Taking a stripper somewhere more private, where you can talk without shouting across a table, where she can lean back against you or sit in your lap, where the lighting is dim, and it's just the two of you, can create the moment you need to move the relationship forward.

Additionally, most clubs won't bother interrupting a dancer who is settled into a private area. This means that she won't be called to stage, or for **STAGE WALKS** (known as **CATTLE CALLS OR SHOWCASES**) or anything else.

As long as you're ponying up the cash, you can mostly keep her all to yourself. Getting down on a private performance is essentially like buying your dancer out of the usual obligation to work the showroom floor, or perform on the stage. For her, this means that you are paying for her to relax a bit while *still getting paid*.

For your purposes, however, the standard lap-grinding dance area will not do. Most clubs these days have some sort of extra personal dance room available, often referred to as a

CHAMPAGNE ROOM, OR VIP SUITE. Whereas the usual dance areas have a set price per song, these VIP dance areas will typically have their own distinct pricing which you'll have to discover at the club you frequent prior to ever deciding to bounce there with a dancer.

PRICE POINTS

A common method to charge for these areas involves a two-step price structure. First, you gain access to the area by making a minimum drink purchase, usually a bottle of Champagne or sparkling wine, hence the name, Champagne Room. This purchase affords you the use of the area for a preset block of time; buying a Champagne room in an hour or half-hour blocks is common.

Some clubs do it this way but without a strict time limit, by simply choosing to send a waitress back to harass you every so often. This ensures a steady stream of expensive alcohol purchases during your stay, and if you taper off or stop altogether, they'll ask you to return to your normal seating.

The second step in the process is paying the entertainer for her time with you. Some clubs will designate a fixed amount that must be paid to the dancer that will accompany you, keyed to the time you wish to spend in the VIP room with her. In this case, using a suite or Champagne room can be little more than an upgraded variation on the traditional private dance area. Other clubs will only insist on the minimum drink purchases, allowing the dancers to set their own prices with their customers.

Letting the girls set their own prices on the top end VIP dances is the way that it is handled in most large clubs with well established, financially stable customer bases. Especially since it's easy to administer and tends to be attractive to the strippers that benefit. Low end clubs will often package the whole deal (booze, use of the area, dancer fee) into a single price point; $200 per half hour, for example.

In the event that the club you are visiting does not serve alcohol, you will usually find that the upgraded suites are offered at a set price that includes both the cost of the dancer, and the use of the room included.

These upgraded dance areas serve to add a level of intimacy with your target stripper, and create opportunities to come across with more money for her. While I'm sure that the concept of enhanced privacy probably sounds Ok to you, the idea that you would be purposefully looking for a chance to spend more money is probably *less attractive.*

Be that as it may, you do need this opportunity to pay her more, regardless of how stupid that might sound. Paying out in a bigger way rewards your girl, justifying her continued investment in your burgeoning connection without worrying that the electricity in her crappy apartment is going to get shut off.

Further, pulling a dancer from the immediate demands of the showroom by paying off the club is a clear proof of your value as a **POSITIVE MALE PRESENCE.** The fact that you are doing this while putting money into her hands as well only serves further to reinforce the point.

While you clearly want to pay girls for their time in the club, you can't become some kind of lame slave who always seeks to make his mistress happy with gifts of money. Your method of paying dancers will have a measured, **STRATEGIC PACING** if you follow the advice in this book. While this works to keep the stripper at your table generally content, and preserves your bankroll, it may sometimes be less conspicuous or convincing than you may wish.

Nonetheless, you shouldn't suddenly break character just to impress the girl with an extra bit of money, especially if you're doing it because some guy with more cash is competing for her attention. What you need is a legitimate excuse for handing over the extra scratch that won't create a counterproductive sense of entitlement within the heart of your intended stripper-girl.

SAFE HAVEN

Taking your girl down on a private suite or Champagne room creates just such a justification while removing her from the competitive environment you share with other customers. Better yet is the fact that getting your target alone in VIP gives you the chance to spend some real quality time in an intimate setting.

While there, you will have effectively isolated her from work demands, friends, other customers, her competitors, and direct disturbance from club staff. This is the time for your girl to get totally **FOCUSED ON YOU**, and to be free of interference

This doesn't mean that things have to get all down-and-dirty in the VIP though. The rules about dancing with your girl still apply here; generally speaking, don't do it. The whole point of bringing her into the private room is not to enable groping her ass or making some kind of creepy blowjob request. You are simply moving to a **VENUE** that allows for privacy, conversation and comfort building.

You don't want to spend inordinate amounts of time here, just make the trip every so often so that you can justify the higher payout, and get some one-to-one time. Quite often when you are out in the main showroom area, your dancer will have some sort of public persona she is projecting, but if you have been working her correctly, she will now have the opportunity to ease back on the throttle with that, if not drop it altogether.

Getting dancer-girl to back off on her stripper bullshit, and start acting in a more relaxed, natural fashion is a primary goal for you here. You surely need to get her to be herself; relaxed, open, and free to make a genuine connection. *Everything* you do out on the showroom floor and at stage side is actually just preparation for time spent alone in VIP.

When you walk into this place with her on your arm, you should feel the relief radiate out from her; you are safe, a good investment of her time, pleasant to be around, and all the meetings up to this point have piqued her curiosity towards you.

Further, she knows that moving to an intimate location will serve as a break for her, and your current track record is an indication that the experience will most likely be agreeable, at least comparable to what she is forced to deal with usually.

Take care as you make this move not to allow a break in character, and start acting like a drunken pervert. Keep everything polite, civil and courteous to whatever extent possible as you settle in. If there is a cocktail server waiting on you, remain generous and respectful with them as they handle your needs; your dancer will always be watching.

Also, pay attention to personal effects, and articles of clothing (like a jacket) to make sure they are secure, out of the way, and unobtrusive. Take whatever time is required, for you and your dancer, to get set comfortably before declaring game-on.

At some point, your girl will either make a move to dance for you, or at least ask if you're ready to begin. You need to decline...politely and *just for now*. Ask instead if she'd be willing to hang out for a while, perhaps taking some time to talk for real now that you are in a better location. Most dancers will have no problem with this request, happy to sit with you while sharing drinks, and the privacy afforded by the dance area.

Don't forget that your mission with this girl is *not* about getting overpriced dances, but is ultimately intended to bring her over into your life, and your bed at some point. You can't go into this worried that if you don't get something in the VIP, that you are somehow wasting your money.

You just have to let that go for now, releasing any concern over the eventual outcome, choosing to focus your energy on the things about this girl that you truly like, the ways in which you derive pleasure from her company, learning about her physical characteristics, and watching her body language.

By now you will have shown that you possess clear social value, and demonstrated that your interest is genuine. In all likelihood, your dancer is already deriving some measure of comfort from your presence. You are gradually becoming the man she wishes were there when you are not, especially when dealing with the other, more typical, customers instead.

You're moving now to the private area of the club, offering a **CHANGED CONTEXT** for your dealings with your target stripper, one free of competition, or distraction. She is **ISOLATED**, and only you may demand her attention.

You must capitalize on the moment without being tied to outcomes or making demands. You cannot be afraid of rejection, only holding in your mind a positive, clear vision in which the two of you are together, and connected in whatever way suits you best, and is most pleasing to your nature and purpose.

Staying within character, congruent with the image you have built in her imagination, you have politely demurred on the offer of an immediate dance within the VIP. While it may not be outwardly visible, try to observe with your mind's eye as your dancer breathes a sigh of relief.

Not, perhaps, that she did not wish to dance for you but that you valued her highly enough to spend money for the chance just to get to know her better, something that could be done for free in the public areas of the club.

LOVELY ROSES

This should increase your value in her estimation; it is the same basic mechanic at work when you buy roses for your wife or girlfriend. Roses are outrageously expensive, and quickly die soon after they are given.

There is no real, practical reason to give someone roses, no matter how pretty or sweet smelling they may be. Yet, any man who has had any experience in love knows that a gift of expensive flowers has clear, demonstrably high value in the eyes of the woman who receives them.

Women all share a desire for security when engaging in **PAIR-BONDING** behavior. Any male willing to offer gifts that are expensive or difficult to acquire, yet are essentially valueless will automatically garner attention from viable females. His behavior suggests that he is willing, and able to expend extra effort on behalf of his chosen female, allowing himself to become committed to her in the process.

> *As an aside here; let's take a moment to look at why this shiny-trinket-acquisition behavior demonstrates commitment on the part of a courting male.*
>
> *Back in the day, like around the time pong became the first home video game, people only got to eat what they killed or gathered themselves.*
>
> *When you wake up every day of your life never knowing where the next double cheeseburger is coming from, it tends to focus you powerfully on survival. For most people, most of the time, there was no time for anything that didn't involve getting fed.*
>
> *Therefore, if you took time out of wooly mammoth hunting to go looking for trick crap to impress girls with, it has two immediate and direct consequences in life:*
>
> **Your chance of accidently starving to death is increased dramatically.**
>
> **Your chance of banging other cave-babes is seriously impaired.**

If you were looking to get down with some female in the group or tribe, you'd be forced to accept both personal risk and limited reproductive opportunities, thus demonstrating that you were one serious motherfucker; in other words, committed.

All human social dynamics continue to operate on basic principles such as this, **even today.**

Demanding useless trinkets and shiny baubles from suitors are one reliable form of reproductive screening that lets sexually active females filter out unsuitable bonding candidates, and focus in on those that offer the most benefits to her, and any potential offspring.

Nothing truly says,

I'm safe

I have a penis

And if you're interested

In me fucking you

I'm available

Quite the way giving a girl a bouquet of lovely roses does.

And it works too because, as I mentioned in an earlier chapter, women are **RAVING PSYCHOTICS**. Spending extra money on something that you could do for free, simply because you appear to enjoy the company of the dancer that benefits from a bounce to VIP could be considered an equally effective method of handing over the expensive trinkets and shiny baubles as giving roses or any other crap like that, if not more.

EXPERT TIPS

These are some notes to help guide you while you're engaged in comfort-building during VIP:

Don't pepper her with questions, it's annoying and can cause defensiveness

Ask strategic questions simply to stimulate her talking, she'll take it from there

Listen genuinely, and watch her non-verbal cues as she speaks

Rely on active listening to move the conversation forward

Sit in the seat so that you can face her

Use casual touch; brush her hair off her shoulder, fix a costume strap, anything

When she seems comfortable, sit again side-by-side, leaning slightly into her

Once you have made full-torso touch by leaning into her, lean slightly away

When you shift away, do it slowly, and allow her to come with you

Put an arm around her without groping

Don't hesitate or ask permission

But always act with class

THE ACTIVE LISTENER

You may have noticed that I made mention of something called **ACTIVE LISTENING** there in the VIP notes. Active listening is that people do with their bodies and voices when they are listening to your crap and want you to know they're participating. You probably see women and all kind of mental health professionals use this method liberally.

You know, people shake their heads, nod, move their hands and arms, and make a lot of expressive nonsense sounds. You'll be talking to somebody and they'll nod their head vigorously to signal you to continue, or suddenly exclaim with some kind of non-relevant nonsense like, *"Ah! Oh, no! What? She didn't do that? No!"*

Meanwhile, you're thinking to yourself,

"WTF are you talking about? You don't even know the person I'm referring to in this story, don't make stupid disapproval sounds about something you know nothing about, you fucking idiot."

Despite how ridiculous active listening can be at times, it is the preferred method of communication for most women. If your dancer is telling you something and you just sit there staring at her, she'll get pretty uncomfortable.

On the other hand, if you were to nod your head at the appropriate moments, make subtle gestures with your hands, laugh when she hits a comic punch line or occasionally look slightly away as if really thinking about that deep shit she just said, you'll most likely reap dividends in terms of an improved relationship.

Plus, women really like a guy they can talk with; he seems more supportive and trustworthy. Remember, you and a female talking is really her talking while you listen; so learn how to listen and you'll win her over.

PRACTICE MAKES PERFECT

Once you get your girl to the point where she will lean into you easily, you should take the opportunity to practice moving her around, changing her position, and accepting direct instruction from you through the simple mechanism of your light touch.

Keeping her talking while maintaining a **TACTILE CONNECTION**, gently guiding her through changes in body position, physical orientation, and location within the VIP area, with nothing more than an easy, light touch, will increase comfort values while maintaining a certain level of sexual tension.

It will also serve as a sort of dress rehearsal for the eventual transition into a fully realized physical relationship. In this way, when your relationship does become overtly sexual in a real sense, it will happen naturally, as the next logical step in a positively evolving relationship.

When you, rehearse with someone,

Role-play with someone, visualize with someone,

Practice with someone, enough times,

As if that someone were, yours already,

Then your practice will eventually become

YOUR REALITY.

In case any of this sounds hard to you, try to keep in mind that most women want a man to lead off, so long as she feels reasonably comfortable with him physically and is relatively confident in his intentions, and capability. In other words, she wants someone to do this with her, and she is biologically programmed to respond appropriately, given the correct **TRIGGER**. You just have to take it a step at a time, and be that trigger.

After all, this is what she wants, and what kind of gentleman would you be if you won't help a lady get what she wants, huh? That's right; you'd be no kind at all. So be a stand-up guy, be a gentleman and *show her the way*. It's what she's waiting for.

Seriously though, if this kind of thing were actually all that difficult, the human race would have probably declined into extinction tens of thousands of years ago. We didn't, and that, therefore, is proof positive that it's fucking easy…mostly in a literal sense. Even with strippers.

Hell, *maybe even easier with them actually*, since all you're actually overcoming with dancers is their deeply rooted suspicion that you're trying to pull some shit on them. Which you *are* in a way, so just get on with it and stop stressing about the whole thing.

The occasional trip to the VIP justifies higher pay outs from you without creating a negative sense of entitlement in your girl. It isolates her from her social support structure, creating opportunities for intimacy, and privacy. Your dancer gets the chance to drop the stripper force-field she carries around all day long, and you get the chance to make an actual, direct connection. It provides the perfect environment for escalated physical contact and gives you both the chance to practice being together.

And what about that private dance I already told you not to get? Whether she dances for you in the VIP will be the basic indicator of your success. Simply put, if you do this VIP thing a time or two, and your paramour is satisfied not dancing for you, then either she is the wrong girl, or you are just fucking it all up.

When you get it right, she'll insist on dancing. It will seem spontaneous. It won't be rough. Her face will be close to you. She'll probably take your hands to show you where it's alright to cross the line. Afterward she may become shy or act embarrassed, *which is exactly what you want*. It's imperative that you capitalize on any situation in the VIP that leads to an expression of sudden modesty by your dancer.

When things get physically heated in some way during VIP, a female who wants that behavior to continue or progress will seek permission. That does not mean that she is going to ask you if it's ok, it's not that kind of permission.

What she needs is consensus with you that none of this is her fault and that nobody could blame her for what's happening. It's a social permission that she's seeking here.

Just take the fall for everything. Don't get crazy and overdo it, but make sure she knows that whatever just happened was totally your fault, that you're sorry if things got out of hand and that you'll be a good boy in the future.

If you can pull off the correct level of contrition, it will grant her **IMMUNITY** from later prosecution as some freaky slut.

Don't be dumb when it comes to giving a girl the go-ahead; grant her the immunity she wants, when she wants it.

CHAPTER 14

No time for time

WHAT HAPPENS TO US IN THE FUTURE? DO WE BECOME ASSHOLES OR SOMETHING?

- Carl Sagan, astronomer, astrophysicist, cosmologist, author of the most popular book ever written in the English language, co-founder of the Planetary Society, helped write the Arecibo Message beamed into space as a greeting to Extra-Terrestrial civilizations on behalf of all humanity; succeeded in making science fun and engaging for billions and billions of people; blamed for most of us now being less stupid.

How fast do you need to make things happen with the stripper you're hoping to win over? Fucking *fast*, and make no mistake about that, brother. The more you and fantasy-girl are exposed to each other in the club, the more secure and comfortable she will become. And, just like any of the other *boy meets girl and then fucking blows it* social situations that afflict guys all over the world with permanent cases of life in the **FRIEND ZONE**, if you wait too long, she will get *too* comfortable.

Once a girl gets too comfortable, she will start genuinely valuing the easy comfort of your non intimate relationship, and not want to ruin it with sex and intimacy. Also, giving her too much time to get comfortable also gives you more than enough time to say or do something that blows her perception of your social value outright.

Crossing into friend territory with a dancer in a strip club has another effect as well, something I'm convinced must be unique to the strip club industry. It gets *weird*. Doing simple shit like sitting next to her while she's in her underwear; carrying on conversation while her bare tits are just a few inches from your face, getting a dance, pretty much anything.

The fun in a strip club derives from the blatant sexual tension that the environment deliberately creates, and that tension relies powerfully on a certain **SUSPENSION OF DISBELIEF** that is fragile as a little kid's soap bubble floating past a thorn bush; the tiniest prick (no pun intended) and...*Pop!*...it's gone like it never was. If you get too friends-y with a stripper, it gets increasingly hard to maintain the sex thing, and once that's gone it's as if you both suddenly realize where you are, and what you're doing. Seriously, it's awkward, and well worth avoiding.

If you take too long to hook your favorite stripper-girl and turn her into your girlfriend with the crazy job, you'll lose the chance altogether. You need to act fast, and decisively to **GENERATE ATTRACTION** with your future girlfriend, achieve a level of comfort that can lower her defenses, and finally, make your move. How long is too long, and how fast is fast?

Well, while the exact definition of too long and fast may vary somewhat in this context, the general consensus is that you need **ABOUT TEN HOURS** or so to get to a point where the relationship can change venues and maybe twice that much time for attraction to turn into friendship.

The guidelines on time here are referring to a dancer's total exposure to you, broken up over several instances. A good rule of thumb is to visit her club about two hours at a time. Visit for much shorter than that, and you'll have little of the time that you need with her. If you spend much more than that at any given time you can end up broke, over intoxicated, in a physical bar fight that will ruin everything even if you win, or simply find yourself becoming over exposed to your girl.

Hanging out too long in the club also has the effect of making you into a creep that spends all his time *lurking around in strip clubs*, or can turn you into a Sucker, always waiting around for your stripper like some pathetic loser. Neither of these conditions is likely to enhance your image as someone a dancer will want to make breakfast for in the morning. Avoid with extreme prejudice whenever possible.

Let's say that you visit the club twice a week, for about two hours per visit. You tend to come in on slower evenings where the demands on a stripper's time are less strenuous, and the overall pace is less hectic. Because the customer traffic is slower, it can be comparatively more difficult to make money on these shifts for the girls.

Not only will this ensure that your dancer has more time to spend on you without hassle, but she will be more focused and attentive to your interaction than if you were to drop in during the busy time. Additionally, because money is scarce on a slow shift, the **RELATIVE VALUE** of what you spend on her will increase dramatically.

This means that, in **NO MORE THAN FIVE WEEKS**, you should be positioned to cross over with your new stripper girlfriend (meeting up for your first legitimate date at the very least) or be prepared to cut bait and move on. If you were to change input variables such as how often you visit her and for how long each time, then you can adjust the overall time accordingly. In my opinion, anything longer than two months is too long, and trying to put in ten solid hours in less than two weeks will force you to become overexposed.

I'm aware that there is some genuinely good, and relatively proven advice out there regarding dating and seduction that says that you can get a girl into bed within 7-10 hours (with which I happen to agree) but that spreading it out over the course of 3-6 weeks is simply an invitation to the competition, or might even be considered outright failure. True enough, when you are talking about normal girls in typical social situations...except that we're not talking about normal girls here.

Strippers are a whole other kind of girl than the one you run into down at the local sports bar, or on Internet dating sites. While they're fundamentally the same in perhaps 80% of the fundamental things that tend to add up to that weird concoction that we call women. It's that other twenty percent that makes them different. It's almost as if somebody went in and ripped out a sizeable chunk of the standard **SOCIALIZATION MECHANICS** that we all learn as we grow up.

Things relating to playing nice with others, the difference between love and sex, certain conceptual fundamentals regarding money, and a working knowledge of how to operate the machinery of Western civilization seem to have just been stripped out, pun totally intended. Into this gaping void has now been inserted all manner of things that are counterproductive, self-destructive, prejudicial, ignorant, or otherwise just not related to reality as we know it.

On the other hand, this volatile blend of urban legends, repressed memories, crap learned from MTV, the back of cereal boxes, and the inside of fortune cookies is often being mixed together and packaged in a physically desirable female.

Attractive females tend, as a general rule, to be in **HIGH SEXUAL DEMAND**; thus they typically have loads of social experience, and usually don't freak out when they see a dick. When you start putting that all together, you most often find a hot chick with an interesting, quirky personality who is damn fun at a party.

The other thing you get is cunning, and plenty of it. **CUNNING** is an attribute that is often associated with serpents, foxes, secret agents, frontier town whores, ninjas, and Paris Hilton. The modern stripper is essentially all of these things at the same time, like a bunch of little Machiavellians in bikinis.

These girls can shock you with an admission that they have no idea where to put a postal stamp on an envelope, or with their total bewilderment regarding why the electricity got turned off just because they didn't pay the bill, then turn around and show you how to get your keys out of a locked car without breaking any windows, save $500 a year by buying your underwear in the garment district, or sneak in and out of bed without making a sound.

Standing by your side in a street brawl, a stripper may draw a knife from her purse that saves your ass, yet have no **CONCEPTUAL FRAMEWORK** with which to grasp the idea that the learning permit she obtained in high school is not the same thing as a driver license.

Essentially, most strippers are criminally intelligent, emotionally crippled, socially expert idiot-savants who don't know jackshit about anything, are used to always getting their way, and come dangerously equipped with hot people bodies. Their motivations are murky, and without regard to accepted **SOCIAL MORES.**

Many dancers have no perceptual ability to grasp basic conventions that most of us take for granted, such as the idea of cause and effect. The average exotic dancer is what you might call a **RANDOM VARIABLE.**

There is truly no theory of social dynamics, or field of anthropological, psychological, or sociological study that can predict what will happen when a random variable is introduced into a stable or predictable system. So, no matter how sophisticated and useful any particular system for picking up chicks may be, or how well it can be demonstrated by its developer, it still will not have universal application where exotic dancers are concerned.

Further, when you take a moment to consider that a stripper's job requires them to fake their emotional states, act extroverted, promiscuous, and to pretend sexual arousal and attraction in order to get money for food...well, *good luck* with applying those systems in any consistent manner.

So, bringing it back to what I said earlier, you have five weeks or less; hitting the club twice a week for a couple of hours at a time. If that's not enough strip club time for your tastes, then just pick a second club and alternate between them. That lets you work two separate dancers who don't know shit about what you're doing, two hours per night, four or five days per week. If you need more club time than that, then perhaps you need counseling or maybe a pleasant evening discussion group down at the local YMCA.

Work fast, stay on your game, and keep it all in perspective.

CHAPTER 15

The morning after

DISREGARD FEMALES, ACQUIRE CURRENCY.

- Benjamin Franklin, author, statesman, ambassador to France, inventor of electricity, lead singer of Metallica.

Ten to twenty hours, that's honestly all you got.

You're going to walk into the local strip joint, pick out a girl, get her attention, and go to work. Over the course of the next few weeks, you will pursue this girl, and probably try many, or even most of the things I have told you about.

You will attempt to use some of the inside knowledge of how clubs work to your benefit, and some of what I have said about exotic dancers themselves will come into play, I'm sure.

And you will crash and burn, *spectacularly* too. Get over it, because this is just the beginning, and if you stick with it, you will get better, become successful, and eventually earn the right for everything to get far, far worse. Right now you're just doing it wrong, trying to follow a formula, and to pace things out just so. In the end, you'll figure out how best to adapt the basic ideas we've discussed here into something that works well for you, something that you can wear naturally, like a second skin.

One of the advantages of being on a timer with the strippers is that it will force you to move your efforts to a new target as the one you've focused on plays out with no positive result. As you shift from dancer to dancer, jump to a new club, or even run multiples in a week, you'll start building a body of experience that will dial you in ever closer to getting the girl you've always dreamed of.

Just a few of the great things about choosing exotic entertainers as your **DRUG OF CHOICE** is that they are paid to be there, will talk to you no matter what, and can be relied on to be lonely, and on the lookout for someone, even if they're not yet sure who that someone might be. In an odd fashion, there may be no other group of girls available who will let you get in there and work it like strippers will, giving you all the opportunity you need to get better at your game until finally you start hitting the bull's eye.

As you keep at it, pursuing the stripper-girl of your dreams, you will be confronted, again and again with their seemingly insurmountable defenses. This in itself is valuable, since each time you deal with their dancer persona, their defensiveness, the lies and misdirection; you'll start learning to see right through it all, to anticipate it, to plan for it, to be prepared.

On the far side of this dancer defense is...**NOTHING**. In almost every case, you'll find just this single layer of barbed wire, trench works, and defensive emplacements with nothing behind it but open, empty ground. Kind of like some *Maginot Line* of the stripper-soul; once you breach it, or flank it, the road lay open to Paris (the one in France.)

It's as if the average dancer is so emotionally vulnerable, that she has subconsciously focused on building up this one impenetrable barrier to keep herself safe to the exclusion of all else; *except that truly nothing is impenetrable*, so once you make it through the wall, you get the run of the place. Once you're in, you're in. It's possible to fuck it up once you make it to this point; guys do it all the time, but honestly, you actually have to work at it.

Once a dancer lets you in, you see, she really, really, really wants to believe. I'm not trying to make the girls sound stupid, and weak, however, it's just that most of them are extremely vulnerable on one level or another, and it's easy to run amok and cause damage that can't truly ever be repaired.

Stay with it, punch through that armor, but you once you do watch where you step, and go easy. **MOST OF THEM, AT HEART, ARE ESSENTIALLY INNOCENT GIRLS THAT JUST WANT TO BE LOVED.** If you take poor advantage of that you'll pay for it, in this life or the next.

Ten to twenty hours, maximum. After that, just say, *fuck it, and drive on.* There are plenty of girls who turn 18-21 every single day, and your local girlie joint gives you plenty of opportunity to meet those of them that are sexy, fun, and **DOWN TO GET DOWN**. Don't get fixated, and don't limit yourself. Repeat after me;

Just say, fuck it and drive on.

FROM BAD TO WORSE

Sometimes things don't always work out though, and you may be wondering about what happens when everything goes to crap. If you haven't taken the time to think that through, then I encourage you do it fully prior to getting deeply involved with one of these girls. Let's run through a few choice examples right now, just to get the general idea down.

The following hypothetical situations are presented in a question and answer format. Simply answer the questions as you go to find out where that particular scenario might end up. I want to stress again that these are examples of really bad situations that you may get in to...but that does not mean they *are* going to happen or that these few examples we're discussing are somehow the limit of possible stripper shenanigans.

A section describing all the obnoxious crap that *could happen* would be a hell of a lot longer than this...Well that would actually be a book all in its own right.

SHE APPEARS TO HAVE A SERIOUS DRUG OR ALCOHOL PROBLEM:

IS REHAB, DETOX OR WHATEVER WORKING?

Yes?

Keep an eye on her around your prescriptions.

No?

Then walk, right now.

SHE CONSTANTLY ASKS FOR CASH:

DO DATES, MEETINGS OR ACTIVITIES REQUIRE THAT YOU SPEND LARGE AMOUNTS OF MONEY?

YES?

You're not in the relationship you thought you were, walk away right now.

NO?

Go to the next question.

DO YOU LIVE TOGETHER?

YES?

She needs help. Handle the finances yourself, teach her money skills, or walk.

NO?

Go to the next question.

IS SHE JUST LOUSY WITH MONEY?

YES?

It won't get better, and you need to walk away before you end up homeless.

NO?

She's playing you; this isn't the relationship you thought it was, so walk.

YOU THINK SHE'S CHEATING ON YOU:

DO YOU HAVE SOME KIND OF VERIFIABLE PROOF?

YES?

That's what you get for looking through her shit you fucking dumbass; now dump her.

NO?

Go to the next question.

HAVE YOU ASKED HER DIRECTLY?

YES?

Go to the next question.

NO?

Stop being a bitch and go ask her directly.

WHEN YOU ASKED, DID SHE CONFIRM, OR DENY?

CONFIRMED?

Well, at least she's an <u>honest</u> cheater. Do you know what an "honest cheater," has in common with other oxymora like *slave wages*, *death benefits* and *fresh frozen?* That's right it's a phrase that makes no fucking sense...so dump her.

DENIED?

Go to the next question.

IS SHE FULL OF SHIT?

YES?

Blow her ass off, delete her number, and switch clubs.

NO?

Go to the next question.

ARE YOU SURE?

YES?

You mean just like you were sure she wasn't fucking anyone else but you?

NO?

Yep, you're right, you have no fucking idea. Please immediately use the following **EMERGENCY PROCEDURE:**

BLOW HER THE OFF, DELETE HER NUMBER, SWITCH CLUBS, CHANGE YOUR OWN LAST NAME AND CELL NUMBER, THE TOWN YOU LIVE IN, THE STATE WHERE THE TOWN IS LOCATED OR THE SOLAR SYSTEM THAT YOU CALL HOME IF THAT'S WHAT IT TAKES TO MOVE THE FUCK ON. DON'T TALK ABOUT IT, ARGUE WITH HER OVER IT OR TRY TO WORK IT OUT; **SHE CAN'T BE FIXED.**

HER EX-BOYFRIEND KEEPS SHOWING UP/CAUSING SHIT:

DID IT HAPPEN ONCE, AND NEVER AGAIN?

YES?

Fine, but be prepared to call the cops next time.

NO?

Go to the next question.

IF IT KEEPS HAPPENING, DOES SHE ALWAYS HAVE TO GO TALK TO THE GUY?

YES?

Great lock the door behind her and never open it again.

NO?

Go to the next question.

DOES SHE WANT THE GUY GONE AS MUCH AS YOU DO?

YES?

Go to the next question.

NO?

Dump her.

ARE YOU WILLING TO FIGHT FOR HER, WHATEVER THAT MIGHT MEAN?

YES?

Sign up for Krav Maga and be ready to call the cops.

NO?

Dump her.

We could go on like this for a while, but I think you get the general idea. You may have also noticed that there is a theme developing here:

Once they fuck you over, they always will, so just walk away while you still can.

I hate to come off on the negative at this point, but it's a subject that merits discussion before you go wandering off to romance some stripper. If they cheat on you, steal from you, use you, won't break off former relationships to focus on you, waste money and base all their happiness off how much more you can provide, I can guarantee that they *will always be that way.*

Better to face the fact that you picked the wrong girl right now, than to find out later. At least if you find out she's not right for you up front, you can get out while you still can and live to fight another day. That may take some **INNER STRENGTH** on your part, but you can do it, *because there is no way to change or fix them.*

STILL BETTER THAN BORING

On a more positive note, stripper girlfriends can be pretty damn *magnificent,* as I stated way back in the beginning of the book. They are fun, independent, like to surprise you with three-way sex, and often can alter your outlook on life, instilling a sense of adventure, awakening a clear purpose or what the hell ever, and sometimes, what the hell ever is just exactly what you need.

To succeed with dancers, you need to have a little bit of willpower, ego, and a positive self-image. You have to be able to say no when the situation calls for it, and have the right judgment to be able to bug out when things can't work out. You shouldn't go around acting like a bully with women, but you can't be so passive that you can be pushed around, and made to eat it either.

Learn to be assertive, to have a **DEFINITE PURPOSE** that drives you, to be focused, and to have the resolve to get shit done. If you dig on strippers, great, but allow them to join you in your life, don't ever make their lives yours. If you ignore that piece of advice, I guarantee that you'll one day regret it, sooner, rather than later.

Remember, that there are literally thousands of strip joints cranking it out in America, and there are hundreds of thousands of strippers hitting the stage and working the pole every night of the week. If the club you go to turns out not to have the right dancer for you, don't settle, just go somewhere else. Keep doing that until you find the girl you actually want, and who wants you back for real, and not just because you're paying her bills, or what the hell ever it is that she does want.

The strip clubs that open up each day are where the party is at, if you're willing to pay. The girls who walk the stages are the main reason the whole thing is fun, and there's nothing wrong with wanting to bring one home with you. Just don't forget that when you take the dancer out of the club, she turns into something that's kind of like a **REAL GIRL**, and if all you want is the fantasy that you saw up there on the stage, you may end up being disappointed.

Get real clear with yourself about what kind of person you want to be hanging out with. Understand the difference between things that you must get in a relationship, and things that are negotiable. You have to be equally clear about things you dislike but can tolerate, and those things which are **DEAL BREAKERS**.

Once you've put this picture together, use it to screen the girls you talk to, and don't settle until you find someone that fits. Though she may only match up most of the way, you're almost guaranteed to wind up happier.

Finally, you will be in a club as you chase down the girl, and clubs are fun, so lighten the fuck up and be fun yourself. And if you can't have a good time while drinking and staring at naked women then your problems may be bigger than the fact that you might be one stripper short when you hit the rack at night. In the end, whatever may come, just take a deep breath, and repeat the following phrase:

> *It is what it is, tomorrow is another day, and everybody comes back again.*

Oh, and don't forget,

ALWAYS SMILE AND TIP.

TRUE QUOTES

In case you're wondering about some of the introductory quotes at the beginning of each chapter, I have included a quick guide both for your edification and to prevent myself from being sued by someone without a sense of humor.

I'll warn you though that nothing in this section truly has anything whatsoever to do with strippers.

These are the quotes, with a chapter by chapter explanation of what truly was said by whom, along with some extra info about the people to whom I had attributed each quotation:

QUOTES: INTRODUCTION

I don't believe it!

Luke Skywalker - True

That is why you fail.

Master Yoda – True

The first of the quotes is, uncharacteristically, accurate. This was taken from a conversation between **LUKE** (Mark Hamil) and **YODA** (Frank Oz) that went down in the film, *STAR WARS, EPISODE 5: THE EMPIRE STRIKES BACK*, as Yoda used the

218

power of the Force to save Luke's star fighter from being lost in the Dagobah swamp.

Almost everything I learned as a kid about growing up and becoming a man that has turned out to be both valid and useful occurred on screen between the time Luke crash landed on Dagobah, and the time he left to rescue his friends from Cloud City on Bespin over the objections of Yoda and Obi-Wan Kenobi.

As a nine year old kid watching Luke run off to get his ass kicked by his own father from a seat in the (at that time) *Mann's Chinese Theater of Hollywood*, I had this sudden realization that there were some things that the adult males in my life either wouldn't, or couldn't explain about being a guy.

These days I know that back then, guys were disconnected, and really just had no idea how to be men themselves, much less how to show young boys how it's done. As a consequence we now have an entire generation of males who are struggling to become *men* in some way other than just their chronological age.

If you happen to have kids of the appropriate age...boys specifically...you should take the time to hook them on the first three Star Wars movies (Episode 4, 5 and 6) and really make sure they get what's happening in the story as Luke is transformed from boy-dreamer into a hero that redeems his father and, in the process, becomes a man himself.

If you're not exactly sure what the fuck I'm talking about or what the hell some stupid Muppet could possibly tell you about manliness, then I recommend looking up the philosophical concept of THE HERO'S JOURNEY on Wikipedia at bare minimum. If you should happen to be a woman, however, I wouldn't bother with that...girls *can't understand this* anymore than I can truly understand your period or inexplicable desire to write your own damn vows when you get married.

Oh, and Luke *did* deserve to have his ass kicked by his Dad...as I'm sure Yoda would have agreed.

QUOTES: CHAPTER 1

ALL YOUR BASE ARE BELONG TO US

Look alive, men. I've got my freak on for recon.

George Armstrong Custer - False

The quote used in this chapter is one of two in the book that are actually from **SKIPPER** (Tom McGrath) of the *MADAGASCAR* films and related television shows.

GEORGE CUSTER'S last words were lost to history since everyone who might have heard what he said was killed right along with him. I assume he must have said something like, *"Fuck, that hurt!"*

I suppose also that it is equally likely that he said something more in line with the vernacular of the time period, something like, *"Ye gods, man! I am slain!"* The actual final words that we do have a verifiable record for, however, were, *"We've caught them napping!"*

The second quote that I attributed to Custer:

Bring the Gatling guns? What for? They're just Indians, lol!

Is also false, as in I made it up based on the fact that Custer did order his battery of Gatling guns to remain behind along with all the cavalry sabers that had been issued to his regiment. Apparently, Custer thought that the gun battery would slow his column (true) and that the additional firepower was both unnecessary (false) and unmanly because seriously, machine guns are unfair (which is the point of having them.)

He was also concerned that the sound of cavalry sabers rattling against saddles would alert his savvy Indian enemy and disrupt the stealth aspect of his attack. This may have been a legitimate concern had stealth been an important factor in an attack that involved 700 troops mounted on horseback, carrying fluttering flags and sounding bugles as they approached from three separate directions...*in broad daylight.*

As it turns out, both machine guns and swords were *exactly* what would have turned the tide of battle...funny, that.

QUOTES: CHAPTER 2

GIRLS, GIRLS, GIRLS

Don't laugh; your daughter might be working here.

A Posted Sign - True

No explanation required.

QUOTES: CHAPTER 3

IF IT DOESN'T MAKE DOLLARS, IT DOESN'T MAKE SENSE

Strippers are people, too. Naked people, who may be willing to pleasure you for a price you negotiate later, behind a curtain in the VIP room.

Alexander Hamilton – False

This quote was actually spoken by **PETER GRIFFIN** as a part of a public service announcement that occurred at the end of an episode of *FAMILY GUY* featuring scenes in a strip club. I'm reproducing the *P.S.A.* in its entirety, below.

Hi, I'm Peter Griffin. You know we've had a lot of laughs tonight, but I'll tell you what's not funny; killing strippers. Strippers are people too, naked people who may be willing to pleasure you for a price you negotiate later behind a curtain in the VIP room. Besides, there's no need to kill them because most of them are already dead inside. Goodnight everyone.

The rest of the **ALEXANDER HAMILTON** attribution is, however, true; particularly the part about dying in the wake of a duel. I did leave out a part about what actually caused the duel, however.

Apparently, Hamilton did so much shit-talking on political rival and Presidential candidate Aaron Burr in the 1800 election season, that not only did Burr lose his bid for the presidency, but also failed at all his other political aspirations, as well.

Hamilton was seriously on Aaron Burr's ass like no other, and in retaliation, Burr outed Hamilton in public regarding his extramarital affairs. Hamilton was so enraged that the honor of his wife had been smeared and that his dirty pantaloons had been aired in public (particularly since he was guilty as charged) that the whole thing ended up with a duel, and Hamilton dead.

Interestingly enough, Burr didn't actually kill Hamilton during the duel, only managing to wing him a bit, but because the United States was already using the health care system that we have today, Hamilton died from infection.

The other thing, about the Founding Fathers being a bunch of bad asses is also true. In reality though, you probably just know Alexander Hamilton as the guy on the ten dollar bill.

QUOTES: CHAPTER 4

CRAZY BITCH

When the world slips you a Jeffrey, stroke the furry wall.

Abraham Maslow - False

This line was spoken by **ALDOUS SNOW** (Russell Brand) in the film, *GET HIM TO THE GREEK*. The "Jeffrey" scene, which also included Jonah Hill, Sean Combs and Colm Meaney, would have made watching the movie well worth it even if everything else sucked...which it didn't.

ABRAHAM MASLOW, on the other hand, was indeed just as I described. Considered the father of Humanistic Psychology and of the concept of self-actualization as a determining force in human development, Maslow first described the Hierarchy of Needs in his 1943 paper, "A Theory of Human Motivation."

It should be noted that Maslow's Hierarchy of Needs has been reinterpreted by motivational speaker and personal development coach Tony Robbins (among others) for consumption by popular audiences as "The Six Basic Human Needs." The chapter *CRAZY BITCH* in this book is based around the version of the Needs as presented by Robbins...mainly because it is simpler, more intuitive, and easier to explain than the in-depth Maslow original.

And, as far as I'm concerned, anybody who is described as mentally unstable during childhood then goes on to become king-fucking-psychologist of the world pretty much knows how to say, *fuck you*, so I guess that part was pretty accurate too.

QUOTES: CHAPTER 5

SHARP DRESSED MAN

Sixty percent of the time, it works every time.

Bill Clinton – False

This line was delivered by **BRIAN FANTANA** (Paul Rudd) in the film, *ANCHORMAN: THE LEGEND OF RON BURGUNDY*, as he explains the aphrodisiac power of the men's cologne, "Sex Panther."

BILL CLINTON, on the other hand, ran the first government budget surplus since before World War II, faced Congress down at his own trial in *their house* and refused to pay them on another occasion until they *made some fucking decisions*, shot up some enemy countries just because they were playing fuck-around, personally issued kill orders on Osama bin Laden before any of the rest of us knew who the hell he was or that something like 9/11 might one day be possible, scored more ass than he knew what to do with, and is considered one of the most popular U.S. Presidents of all time.

Bill Clinton was a pimp.

QUOTES: CHAPTER 6

LOVE MACHINE

I'm in love with a stripper.

Thomas Otway – False

I'M IN LOVE WITH A STRIPPER is actually a song from the rapper **T-PAIN**...you know, the guy who made use of a harmonizer standard there for about a minute in the music business.

THOMAS OTWAY did, however, write a comedic farce called *THE SOLDIER'S FORTUNE* in 1681, in which he managed to coin the term, **STRIPPING**, to describe a woman getting naked for money. He is also famous (somewhat) for the manner of his death. Apparently, Thomas had not found financial success as a writer and toward the end was reduced to begging.

According to the story, one day while pestering innocent passersby for spare change, some Good Samaritan dropped enough cash on T-Way to go buy some bread; which he promptly did...only to choke to death as he ate *way too fast*, because he was hungry and begging for food and because life is fucking cruel like that some times.

One can only hope that, as a writer, Thomas would have appreciated the irony.

QUOTES: CHAPTER 7

JACKASS

I came here to kick ass and chew bubblegum...and I'm all outta bubblegum.

Theodore Roosevelt – False

This quote appears in the John Carpenter film *THEY LIVE*, and was uttered by **GEORGE NADA** ("Rowdy" Roddy Piper of World Wresting fame) the main protagonist of what was arguably Carpenter's best film.

Despite shitty effects, crappy 80s soundtrack and poor acting, *THEY LIVE* may even be one of the greatest films of all time for its super awesome subtext. Keith David, the guy who does the voice over for all the Navy recruiting commercials, was also in this one as George's best friend, Frank.

TEDDY ROOSEVELT did not ever use a catch phrase involving bubble gum, but he did use another famous one, *"Speak softly and carry a big stick,"* to describe his philosophy on foreign affairs.

Not only were Roosevelt's views on the subject compelling in his own time, but they have been adopted as the de facto policy stance of every U.S. President from then until now.

Roosevelt was a Progressive Republican back when that actually meant something, the youngest President ever to hold office, was the primary force behind the construction of the Panama Canal, and sent America's "Great White Fleet," around the world to scare the shit out of everybody.

The character of **COLONEL WILLIAM LUDLOW** (played by Anthony Hopkins) in the film *LEGENDS OF THE FALL* was loosely patterned after Roosevelt.

If you were in some deep shit, but were somehow allowed to pick any three U.S. Presidents, living or dead, to come to your aid, this is the guy you should probably pick first. And no, I'm not sure what type of deep shit situation that could be, but I'll assume that it involves aliens somehow.

If not aliens, then certainly robots or maybe Canadians...whatever, go with Roosevelt first, he was a big-game hunter and liked guns.

QUOTES: CHAPTER 8

HOUSE RULES

All you have to do is follow three simple rules. One, never underestimate your opponent. Expect the unexpected. Two, take it outside. Never start anything inside the bar unless it's absolutely necessary. And three, be nice.

Dalton's Law – False

This one is actually a line belonging to **JAMES DALTON** (Patrick Swayze) in the movie *ROAD HOUSE*, a contracted bouncer "expert" brought in by the owner of the Double Deuce night club to train the crappy security staff. Somehow this ends up with Patrick Swayze ripping some guy's throat out, a dude with a cowboy hat, a dead guy and money. I'm not sure why any of that was going on though, I honestly wasn't paying attention.

The real *DALTON'S LAW* is an empirical law related to the molecular pressure of gas in confined space, and that was formulated by **JOHN DALTON** in the 19th century. The Wikipedia entry for Dalton's Law has this to say:

In chemistry and physics, Dalton's law (also called Dalton's law of partial pressures) states that the total pressure exerted by the... blah blah blah fiddligibit da duh this shit goes on for a really long time da blah dum do blah blah stuff and things blah blah... by John Dalton in 1801 and is related to the ideal gas laws.

I love it when people get all science-y. I also love it when people say things like, *"ideal gas laws,"* with a straight face, but that's because honestly I'm just an immature child inside. Honestly, I just used this because it was funny (for me) to think of this old Limey chemist from back in the day working the door at some shit hole night club.

Also because something about the behavior of gases in a confined space under pressure reminds me of those nights working at the club when you just knew something awful was about to happen. Oh, and the fact that he and Patrick Swayze's character shared the last name.

Actually it was mostly the last name thing.

QUOTES: CHAPTER 9

THE GENTLEMAN CALLER

Now, a question of etiquette...As I pass, do I give you the ass or the crotch?

Abraham Lincoln – False

TYLER DURDEN (Brad Pitt) delivered this line as he left his airplane window seat and stepped past "The Narrator" (Edward Norton) seated on the aisle, in the film *FIGHT CLUB*. It seemed appropriate.

ABRAHAM LINCOLN is the guy best known for ending slavery, being the dude on the five dollar bill and pennies and getting himself assassinated at the theater. Or, at least that's what most people learned about him in high school. In reality though, he didn't actually end slavery (the 13th Amendment to the Constitution did that) although that was certainly the result of the Civil War which was the defining issue of the Lincoln presidency.

Lincoln was the ultimate political pragmatist in the service of a higher goal: the preservation of the Union and of the republicanism of the Founding Fathers. This is an excerpt of a letter from Lincoln to Horace Greely, the influential editor of the New York Tribune:

My paramount object in this struggle is to save the Union and is not either to save or to destroy slavery. If I could save the Union without freeing any slave I would do it, and if I could

233

save it by freeing all the slaves I would do it; and if I could save it by freeing some and leaving others alone I would also do that. What I do about slavery and the colored race, I do because I believe it helps to save the Union; and what I forbear, I forbear because I do not believe it would help to save the Union. . . .I have here stated my purpose according to my view of official duty; and I intend no modification of my oft-expressed personal wish that all men everywhere could be free.

Lincoln had a view of post-war Reconstruction that would have offered generous terms to the former Confederate States, pardoned almost everyone, allowed the South to accept their defeat with honor and dignity intact, and led to massive investment to repair the damage caused by years of war.

Many historians believe that "Moderate Reconstruction," as Lincoln advocated, would have eased racial tension, leading to the normalization of relations between black and white Americans. In addition, the southern states would have become culturally and economically integrated with the north, resulting in greater equality and prosperity for all.

After his assassination, however, the hard liners in Congress where able to get their way, pushing through what is referred to today as Radical Reconstruction, a generally jacked up policy that directly resulted in Jim Crow laws, racial segregation, extreme poverty, Ned Beatty squealing like a pig in Deliverance and NASCAR.

Despite how everything turned out, Lincoln held the country together through the absolute worst crisis we have ever confronted together as a nation. Almost everyone in this country, North and South, fucking hated Lincoln, including his own blundering Army commanders and the Republican Party establishment that had elected him in the first place, yet somehow he managed to keep the special interests at bay, exert direct, daily control over the military, force Congress to support him and win reelection to a second term by a huge margin.

And he did it all because he didn't give a fuck about anything besides keeping the United States together as one nation.

Lincoln is widely considered by historians and political scientists to be the greatest U.S. President of all time, ranked number one of the top five presidents (in order from first to fifth: Abraham Lincoln, Franklin Roosevelt, George Washington, Thomas Jefferson and Theodore Roosevelt.)

He is also the second guy to pick for your three man team of Dead Presidents in the event of alien invasion, robot uprising or Canadian shenanigans. He was a big, lanky guy with serious reach, and did whatever it took to get the job done.

From his second inaugural address, just a few days before his death:

With malice toward none; with charity for all; with firmness in the right, as God gives us to see the right, let us strive on to finish the work we are in; to bind up the nation's wounds; to care for him who shall have borne the battle, and for his widow, and his orphan—to do all which may achieve and cherish a just and lasting peace, among ourselves, and with all nations.

QUOTES: CHAPTER 10

IT'S NOT JUST A CITY IN CHINA

CHEERS MATE!

Not an acceptable form of tipping in the State of Texas.

A Posted Sign – True

This would be another time where no explanation is required, just enjoy it for what it is.

QUOTES: CHAPTER 11

REWARDS FOR GOOD BEHAVIOR

I aim to misbehave.

Captain Malcolm Reynolds - True

MALCOLM REYNOLDS (Nathan Fillion) was captain of the *"Serenity"* on the Joss Whedon (*Buffy the Vampire Slayer, Dollhouse, Avengers*) TV show, FIREFLY. At the time the show premiered on Fox, it was being promoted by the network as, *"A western in space,"* and frankly, that sounded lame.

I didn't bother to watch and neither did the rest of the country, so the series ended up canceled after just 14 episodes. However, due to the wonders of Netflix, I recently got the opportunity to watch the entire series as well as the later series finale feature film, SERENITY. On behalf of all of people out there who became such die-hard fans of that show in such a short time, allow me to say:

Fuck you Fox, for only giving us fourteen episodes, just...*fuck you.*

QUOTES: CHAPTER 12

AFFORDABLE PLEASURES

This next game was invented by double-jointed Hungarian acrobats from the Munich circus.

P.T. Barnum – False

In my earlier *"Custer"* quote, I mentioned that it was the first of two times I was using a line from **SKIPPER** (Tom McGrath) of the MADAGASCAR films and PENGUINS OF MADAGASCAR TV show. This, obviously, is the other one...because the Penguins are super hilarious to me, (I am both retarded and have a toddler) so sue me. Anybody who can seriously pull off, *"Chimichangas!"*, *"Jumbo Shrimp!"*, or *"Great Hoover Dam!"* as credible exclamations can count on my vote at election time.

The attribution, however, refers to **PHINEAS TAYLOR (P.T.) BARNUM**, the legendary American showman who brought us the *Ringling Brothers and Barnum & Bailey Circus,* amongst other things.

Barnum introduced us to the freak show as an art form, built the first aquarium in the United States, founded the infamous *Barnum's American Museum,* perfected the use of wax museums, founded theaters, sponsored travelling entertainment troupes and famous singing acts, visited with European royalty while he toured with the freak performer Tom Thumb, and ended up buying William Shakespeare's house.

Barnum unquestionably created the whole concept of over the top entertainment and the mind-boggling promotional efforts he used to put asses in seats are in many ways standard today. His use of freak shows, for example, were never the point in their own right, they simply served to attract customers to his museums, shows or whatever else.

Just so in modern strip joints, as the girls aren't actually the point from a business model standpoint, they are simply the freaks that bring customers in the door, willing to pay ridiculous prices on virtually anything and everything.

Barnum is popularly credited with the famous saying, *"There's a sucker born every minute,"* which, as it turns out, he did not say. It is believed that it was actually Michael Cassius McDonald, a Chicago bounty broker, saloon and gambling-house keeper, eminent politician, and dispenser of cheating privileges who is responsible for this aphorism.

Supposedly, it was attributed to Barnum by his circus business archrival, Adam Forepaugh, in a newspaper interview as a way of making Barnum look like an asshole to his customers. Listed next are some things Barnum did say:

The noblest art is that of making others happy.

Without promotion something terrible happens... Nothing!

Nobody ever lost a dollar by underestimating the taste of the American public.

All of which, as far as I can see, remain true today. In the end, P.T. evolved into a respectable businessman, a best-selling author, a noted debunker of snake oil salesmen and spiritual mediums, an elected legislator, anti-slavery reformer, local public official and philanthropist.

I can't think of anyone better suited to being the patron saint of strip joint owners and managers everywhere than Phineas Taylor Barnum.

QUOTES: CHAPTER 13

THERE'S NO SEX IN THE CHAMPAGNE ROOM

What extras do you do in the Champagne Room?

None.

What do you mean by none?

Overheard Conversation – True

Honestly, customers say the darnedest things.

QUOTES: CHAPTER 14

NO TIME FOR TIME

What happens to us in the future? Do we become assholes or something?

Carl Sagan - False

This one is from **MARTY MCFLY** (Michael James Fox) in the film *BACK FROM THE FUTURE,* the sequel to the original *BACK TO THE FUTURE*.

Obviously, **CARL SAGAN** never said this, or if he did, it was probably in private. Sagan was a best-selling author of pop-science books, but was probably best known for his part in the television series *COSMOS* in which he starred and co-wrote.

He is also credited with pioneering the field of exobiology (the study of alien life) and for bringing considerable energy and support for the SETI project (Search for Extra Terrestrial Life.) Through television, movies, books, and lectures he was able to get people excited about science while also introducing the idea of *skeptically scientific inquiry* into American culture.

While I'm not generally what you'd call a science guy, Sagan's ability to communicate a true and beautiful belief in a wondrous and awesome cosmos is truly inspirational, and I think he's an American hero. My discussion here of Sagan is brief, but that's not because there isn't anything to say.

Instead, the scope and impact of the life of Carl Sagan is so powerful that I suppose that any of my typical smart ass ridiculousness would just seem...blasphemous, I guess. So this time I'll just pass on it and say,

Thanks, Carl.

QUOTES: CHAPTER 15

THE MORNING AFTER

Disregard females, acquire currency.

Benjamin Franklin – False

This is actually the definitive version of the **JOSEPH DUCREUX / ARCHAIC RAP** internet meme. Joseph was an 18th century French artist known for his unorthodox painting style, particularly of his own self-portraits. Several of his paintings have been turned into poster macros that allow you to add your own captions.

The *DISREGARD FEMALES, ACQUIRE CURRENCY* variant is taken from **NOTORIOUS B.I.G'S** 1995 hit single *GET MONEY*, in which the lyrics, *"Fuck bitches, get money,"* are featured. Other humorous versions of this meme include:

Do not despise the racketeer, despise the sport.

Don't hate the player, hate the game.

FROM THE ICE-T SONG, "DON'T HATE THE PLAYA."

Gentlemen, I inquire, who hath released the hounds?

Who let the dogs out?

BAHA MEN, FROM THEIR BEST-SELLING CD SINGLE

244

For some reason, the current iterations of this meme are focused on films in which the actor **STEVE BUSCEMI** has appeared:

Fornicate with it my good man, let us go crashing ninepins.

> Fuck it dude, let's go bowling.

DONNY (Steve Buscemi) IN THE BIG LEWBOWSKI

Are thee cognizant of this device? 'Tis the kingdom's smallest violoncello, performing solely for the serving-wenches.

> Do you know what this is? It's the world's smallest violin, playing just for the waitresses.

MR. PINK (Steve Buscemi) IN RESERVOIR DOGS.

A **MEME**, by the way, is a self-replicating idea, usually spread via the internet. Basically, a meme works on the human brain in the same way that a virus works on a computer. What happens is that you view, read or hear the meme without knowing what it is, and the idea creates something known as a **TRANS-DERIVATIONAL SEARCH PATTERN (TDS)** in which your conscious mind attempts to match what it has just experienced with some type of known meaning...except that it can't, because the information is either meaningless, open to too many possible interpretations or just downright wrong in some way.

> *Remember the river dancing girl in the beginning of the book?*

This causes your conscious mind to go into a momentary fuzzy reset mode, thus creating an opening through which the idea is accepted as a fact that makes no sense. People successfully exposed to a meme will usually be consumed by the thought for some period of time lasting up to several days.

Then without warning, the idea and everything that went with it will suddenly disappear from your mind as if it had never even existed at all. This is because you have unconsciously accepted this insensible idea as a fundamental part of reality without any further need for rational consideration.

In other words, your unconscious mind simply says *fuck it* and gives up on figuring out what the hell it's supposed to mean. The meme is then incorporated into the basic structure of how you view the world, interpret information and construct reality.

Memes have been around forever, and are a mainstay of every successful marketing campaign you've ever been exposed to. Memes used in advertising are the reason why you ask for a **COKE** when what you actually want is a *cola flavored soda* or use the term **FEDEX** to mean *shipping something overnight.*

The internet, however, has caused the introduction of memes to explode in scope and reach. The title of Chapter 1 in this book is itself a result of one of the most oddly successful internet memes ever created; just look it up on Wikipedia or you can *Google it* (that was another meme) and you'll see what I mean.

Memes aside, however, **BENJAMIN FRANKLIN** did not ever say "*Disregard females, acquire currency,*" despite the fact that he was well known for his quotes and aphorisms. Franklin was one of the Founding Fathers (as I'm sure you already know) and a polymath, or as we say today, a *Renaissance Man*.

That means he was considered an expert at multiple fields of study and discourse. An example of what I mean by that would be if you were the world's best surgical doctor and a champion race car driver and an astronaut and an award-winning poet and a professional surfer while also being a leading advocate for the homeless. A famous fictional polymath is **TONY STARK** (Robert Downey, Jr.) as depicted in the **IRON MAN** superhero franchise.

Franklin also *did not* invent **ELECTRICITY** since it's a natural fucking phenomenon. He did, however, contribute enormously to our understanding of how electricity works with his experiments with lightning. He also *did* manage to invent all kinds of useful shit though, like lightning rods, bifocals, the *Franklin stove* and the odometer.

A notable journalist, publisher and author, Franklin is still famous for the publication of *POOR RICHARD'S ALMANAC*. He served as ambassador to France during the Revolution and was able to secure the French military assistance that proved invaluable to bringing the war to an end.

And, while he was in France working for our independence, it would seem that he also got like a boatload of French ass...or at least that's how I understand it.

Despite how many groupies he may have had, Franklin was not, to my knowledge, ever the lead singer of the band

METALLICA; that honor goes to **JAMES HETFIELD,** who also did not invent electricity.

As far as I know.

THE STRIP CLUB DATING SURVIVAL GUIDE
HOW TO DATE ANY EXOTIC DANCER & SURVIVE TO TELL THE TALE

FOR MORE TALES OF SURVIVAL, GO TO
WWW.RAWKMODE.COM

YOU DON'T HAVE TO GO HOME, BUT YOU CAN'T STAY HERE.

Printed in Great Britain
by Amazon.co.uk, Ltd.,
Marston Gate.